BETTY A. BLUE is Professor of Spanish and Head of the Foreign Language Department at Southern Arkansas University. She has combined her profession and her hobby—cooking—through the translation of the original Spanish recipes into a simplified version for **Authentic Mexican Cooking**. She has previously published several articles and a foreign language textbook.

CREATIVE COOKING SERIES

AUTHENTIC MEXICAN COOKING

Auténtica cocina de Méjico

BETTY A. BLUE

A SPECTRUM BOOK

PRENTICE-HALL, INC., Englewood Cliffs, New Jersey 07632

Library of Congress Cataloging in Publication Data

Blue, Betty A
   Authentic Mexican cooking—Authentica cocina de Méjico.

   (A Spectrum Book)
   Includes indexes.
1.   Cookery, Mexican.   I. Title   II. Title: Authen-
tica cocina de Méjico.
TX716.M4B58   641.5'972   77-23355
ISBN 0-13-054106-0
ISBN 0-13-054098-6 pbk.

A Spectrum Book

10   9   8   7   6   5   4   3   2   1

Printed in the United States of America

PRENTICE-HALL INTERNATIONAL, INC., London
PRENTICE-HALL OF AUSTRALIA PTY. LIMITED, Sydney
PRENTICE-HALL OF CANADA, LTD., Toronto
PRENTICE-HALL OF INDIA PRIVATE LIMITED, New Delhi
PRENTICE-HALL OF JAPAN, INC., Tokyo
PRENTICE-HALL OF SOUTHEAST ASIA PTE. LTD., Singapore
WHITEHALL BOOKS LIMITED, Wellington, New Zealand

TO

Lynn Purdue
Rhonda Barnard
Nancy Nichols
Ricarda Gean

Photos by:

Charles S. Miers
George Howard Price
Jeanne Lehman

contents

preface

The average person living north of the Rio Grande River has no idea of the marvelous tastes available to him in the nearest of the world's three great cuisines, the one waiting for him just south of the border. In all probability his idea of Mexican food is driving up to one of the local fast-food franchisers and ordering a taco.

After sixteen years of living in Mexican homes and collecting some of their best recipes, I decided that something should be done to correct the popular misconceptions in this country about what the Mexicans actually eat. And since I derive such pleasure from their cuisine, I want to share my enjoyment in preparing it and appreciating it with others.

The weights and measures in these recipes were originally given in the metric system. In the translation from the original spanish, and for the convenience of the reader, these weights and measures have been converted into the system currently used in the United States; a conversion table to the metric system is available in the back of the book.

The multi-course meal usually served between 1:30 and 2:30 in the afternoon is called the "comida." This meal always starts with soup; this is followed by dry soup, then vegetables; the main course consists of fish (habitually on Wednesdays and Fridays), meat, or poultry; and the meal ends with a dessert. Following this enormous meal, one normally takes a siesta or nap.

Mexican cooking is a delightful combination of the cuisine of the Spanish conquerors and that of the native Indians. Only in Peru did the conquistadores find as advanced a culture as they did in Tenochtitlán (now Mexico City), then at the height of the Aztec civilization, and the major portion of that word "civilization" meant food. One of our best sources of information concerning life in Tenochtitlán comes from one of the soldiers, Bernal Díaz del Castillo, who accompanied Hernando Cortés on the conquest of Mexico. Although Díaz del Castillo was only a boy at the time and did not write his **Chronicles** until he was eighty-four years old and had lost his sight and hearing, his recollections are truly remarkable. He tells us about the huge plaza where every class of merchandise was sold, including cacao, vegetables, fowl, fish, meat (even that of young dogs), and all types of fruits. Some of the food, like honey cakes and other sweets, were sold already prepared.

Montezuma, who was the great emperor of the Aztecs at the time of the conquest, had over thirty different dishes prepared by his cooks for every meal. These were placed on small pottery braziers to keep them from getting cold. Every day they cooked chicken, turkey, pheasant, partridge, quail, tame and wild duck, venison, wild pig, rabbits, pigeons, and many other varieties of birds. And at each meal, beautiful Indian women served the emperor tortillas made from corn and eggs.

Since the Spanish had been living under the Arab influence for nearly a thousand years when Columbus discovered America, they brought sugar cane, wheat, rice, bananas, mangos, garlic, onions, and all types of herbs like lemon balm, mint, basil, sweet marjoram, thyme, and rosemary to the new world. And it was Bernal Díaz himself who brought seven orange seeds to Mexico, thus opening the door of the continent to oranges.

The cuisine of Mexico is a part of its culture. Corn, chiles, tomatoes, and beans were the basis of the ancient Aztec and Mayan civilization, and they are still the most important foods of present-day Mexico. Tortillas, the staple of the Mexican diet, are prepared the way the Indian woman ground them out at the time of the Spanish conquerors. Tortillas are a must at every walk of life. They are served in the finest restaurants and the wealthiest homes, and they can be purchased in one form or another from street vendors. The cooking has been influenced by the same factors that determined the language, social structure, government, history, and religion of Mexico.

Ahead of you is a delightful experience in the culinary art of Mexico: an art that mixes two worlds—those of the native Indian and the Spanish conqueror.

!Buen Apetito!

los aperitivos

1

appetizers and canapés

Cocktail parties in Mexico are eating as well as drinking events. Tortillas, toasted or fried in deep fat, are served spread with beans, shredded meat and cheese, or with avocado dip livened with Mexican sauce.

Coctel de Jaibas

Crab Cocktail

There are two types of crabs available at the market, the hard-shell and the soft. Although both types may be of the same species, the soft-shell crabs are caught during the moulting season. This recipe is for the hard-shell variety.

Boil enough water (to which lemon juice, salt, and pepper has been added) to cover four large crabs. Put the live crabs in the boiling water; cover the pan, and boil for fifteen or twenty minutes or until the crabs are a red color.

Remove the crabs from the boiling water and allow them to cool in cold water. Crack the claws open and take out the meat; remove the tail. Force the upper and lower shells apart; take the meat out but save the upper shell of the crab for serving the cocktail. Wash and dry the four shells. Chop the fresh-cooked crab meat into bite-size pieces or substitute 1-1/2 cups canned crab meat.

To make the sauce:

20 asparagus tips, or substitute 1 package frozen tips · 4 tablespoons lemon juice · 6 tablespoons butter · 3 egg yolks · salt · paprika ·

If you are using frozen asparagus tips, follow the directions on the package. For fresh, tie the asparagus tips in a bunch. Cook standing upright on a rack with just enough boiling water to cover the rack. Cover the pan and steam cook for fifteen minutes. Drain the tips, reserving liquid.

In a double boiler, stir the lemon juice with the 6 tablespoons of melted butter. Season to taste with salt and paprika. Gradually add the slightly beaten egg yolks mixed with a little hot broth from the cooked asparagus tips. Cook over low heat for several minutes, stirring constantly until the mixture begins to thicken. Mash the asparagus tips and combine them with the sauce; or, for a smoother sauce, blend in the blender.

Put individual servings of crab meat in the shell and serve hot with the asparagus topping.

SERVES 4.

Coctel de Camarones

Shrimp Cocktail

1 cup catsup or chili sauce · 2 tablespoons horseradish · tabasco or hot sauce to taste · salt and pepper to taste · 2 pounds of shrimp · 1 celery stalk (chopped) · 1/3 cup sliced onion · lettuce ·

For 6 servings allow 2 pounds of fresh shrimp, two 12-ounce packages of frozen shrimp, or 3 cups of canned shrimp.

Prepare a cocktail sauce with one cup of catsup or chili sauce, 2 tablespoons of horseradish, a few drops of Tabasco or other commercial hot sauce, and salt and pepper to taste. Refrigerate.

Combine one quart of water, the stalk of celery, onion, and 3 thin slices of lemon. Bring to a boil; add the fresh shrimp; bring to a second boil; turn off the heat and let stand 6 to 8 minutes. Cool and remove the shells. (Canned shrimp may be substituted; or you may use frozen shrimp prepared according to the directions on the package.) Refrigerate.

Place a lettuce leaf in each serving cup; add half a dozen or so of the chilled shrimp; top with a heaping tablespoon of cocktail sauce. Garnish with lemon wedges and serve.

SERVES 6.

Coctel de Ostiones

Oyster Cocktail

Prepare the same cocktail sauce (which is enough for 4 dozen oysters) as in the preceding shrimp cocktail recipe; refrigerate several hours before serving.

If you are preparing oysters that are still in the shell, scrub the shells thoroughly and rinse under cold water. Insert a strong knife into the unhinged side of the oyster shell, and cut through the muscle which holds the two halves together. Reserve one of the shell halves for serving each oyster.

Serve the oysters in their individual shells on a bed of cracked ice. Serve the sauce in the center of the platter or in a side dish.

Allow 6 to 8 oysters per person. 4 dozen oysters should serve 6 people.

Anchoas a la Vinagreta

Anchovies in Vinegar Sauce

filets of anchovies (1 can) · 3 hard-boiled eggs · parsley · olive oil · vinegar · pepper ·

Arrange the anchovies flat in the form of a lattice on a platter. Sprinkle them with diced hard-boiled eggs, the well-chopped parsley, a little oil, vinegar, and pepper, and serve. (This makes an excellent topping for a lettuce salad if one so desires.)

SERVES 6.

Huevos con Camarones

Eggs with Shrimp

4 eggs · salt · 8 cooked shrimp · mayonnaise ·

Hard boil the eggs; remove the shells and cut in half lengthwise. Remove the yolks; add a little salt and mayonnaise and mix thoroughly with a fork.

Fill the whites with the yolk mixture and on each one, place a shrimp (canned or frozen shrimp may be used). Add a little more mayonnaise to each shrimp and chill in the refrigerator for an hour or two before serving.

MAKES 8.

Canapés

Canapé is a French word which has been adopted into the Spanish by use of the word "costron" from "costra" meaning crust. A "costron" is bread which may be cut in small squares, circles, diamonds, or other shapes and deep fat fried in either olive oil or vegetable oil. Each "costron" then may be garnished with one of a variety of spreads. One cup of spread should cover from 24 to 36 small canapés.

Any of the following canapé recipes may be served on fried bread or on your favorite crackers.

Canapé de Caviar

Caviar Canapés

Combine 1/4 cup of black caviar with one teaspoon of lemon juice and 1/4 teaspoon of diced onion. Serve on fried bread crusts or cocktail crackers; or fill the whites of hard-boiled eggs cut lengthwise with this mixture and serve cold. Will make 12 small canapés or fill six halves of hard-boiled eggs.

Canapé de Pollo o Pavo

Chicken or Turkey Canapés

Grind one cup of cooked chicken or turkey meat and add enough mayonnaise to spread easily on fried bread squares or cocktail crackers. Season with salt and pepper. Garnish each canapé with diced celery. Will make from 24 to 36 small canapés.

Canapé de Jamón

Ham Canapés

Grind one cup of cooked ham and add enough mayonnaise to spread easily on fried bread. Cover the bread with mustard before adding the ham mixture. Serve with 6 hard-boiled eggs cut in halves lengthwise and garnish the platter with parsley. Will make from 24 to 36 canapés.

Canapé de Hongo

Mushroom Canapés

Chop 1/2 pound of mushrooms and sauté them in butter for a few minutes. Season with salt and pepper to taste and serve on fried bread.

Canapé de Langosta de Mar

Lobster Canapés

Mash cooked or canned lobster to a paste; add enough mayonnaise to spread easily. Add a few drops of lemon juice, and spread on cocktail crackers or fried bread squares. Garnish the canapé with chopped parsley.

Canapé de Camarón

Shrimp Canapés

Follow the preceding recipe for Lobster Canapés, substituting shrimp for the lobster. These are delicious topped with little pieces of cooked shrimp. Garnish with a border of finely chopped parsley.

las bebidas

2

One of the most popular misconceptions about Mexican cuisine is that tequila is the national drink; actually, the national drink is pulque, the fermented juice from the maquey plant. Pulque is the same now as it was when Cortés and his men arrived in Tenochtitlán. History tells us that this drink was the downfall of the Toltec empire. Whether or not this is true, pulque can be purchased today in every village or city, dispensed from large glass barrels on portable stands or carts. Mexicans consume more pulque than water.

Pulque de Arroz

Rice Pulque

2 pounds of long grain rice · 4 pounds of granulated sugar · 1 large pineapple, peeled and chopped · 6 ounces almonds, blanched and ground · 6 cloves ·

Soak the rice in a pot with one quart of water and two pounds of brown sugar. Cover the pot well. Leave at room temperature in a place where there is little sun for six days. Then uncover it and add the crushed cloves. Cover it again. After another six days, add another two pounds of sugar, six quarts of water, the crushed pineapple, and almonds.

Strain the following day and serve over ice. Will keep in the refrigerator indefinitely.

MAKES 1-1/2 GALLONS.

Pulque Curado de Melón

Cured Melon Pulque

1 quart pulque ·
1 medium ripe
cantaloupe ·
6 ounces sugar ·
1 whole clove ·
1 whole black
peppercorn ·
1 cinnamon stick ·

Peel and chop the melon; add the spices and half of the sugar. Strain through a coarse cloth and add the strained pulque and the remaining sugar. Leave at room temperature for two hours before serving. Serve at room temperature or over ice.

SERVES 6 (8 OUNCE GLASSES).

Pulque de Almendra

Almond Pulque

1 quart pulque ·
3 oranges ·
4 ounces almonds,
blanched and
ground · 1 cup
sugar ·

Mix the pulque with the ground almonds, the sugar, and the juice of 3 oranges; let stand for three hours; strain, and let stand two hours more before serving. In Mexico, this drink is served at room temperature. You may prefer it over ice. Will keep in the refrigerator indefinitely.

SERVES 6.

Coco Fizz

Coconut Fizz

2 cups coconut milk
· 2 cups gin ·
2 lemons ·
4 tablespoons
granulated sugar ·

Frozen coconut milk is available in some supermarkets. To make your own, combine 2-1/2 cups of canned coconut with 2-1/2 cups of milk. Refrigerate about 2 hours; then blend in an electric blender for one minute. Pour through a strainer until the yield is two cups.

Mix the coconut juice, gin, sugar, and lemon juice well; shake in a cocktail shaker with a little chopped ice. Serve in small glasses, putting in three parts of this drink to one part club soda.

SERVES 10 (4 OUNCE GLASSES).

We may think of eggnog as a special drink for the holiday season, but this is not true in Mexico. Eggnog—called "rompope" there—is served at every season of the year and in all parts of the country.

Rompope

Eggnog

6 cups milk · 4 cups sugar · 10 whole cloves · ground nutmeg · 30 egg yolks, well beaten · 2-inch stick of cinnamon · 3 cups of brandy ·

Cook the milk with the cloves and cinnamon. When it first boils, add the sugar and take from the fire without stirring it.

When it begins to cool, stir with a wooden spoon to dissolve the sugar; beat the egg yolks. When the milk is completely cool, strain it, and mix in the yolks. Put into a large container and add the brandy gradually, beating thoroughly. Let the foam go down; then chill. Rompope is better if it is refrigerated several weeks before serving. Serve cold in small liqueur glasses. Sprinkle each serving with ground nutmeg.

MAKES 12–14 CUPS.

Rompope Almendrado

Almond Eggnog

6 cups milk · 6 egg yolks, well beaten · 2 whole cloves · 1 tablespoon vanilla · 1 cup sugar · 3/4 cup almonds, blanched and ground · 3 cups aguardiente, brandy, or bourbon

Boil the milk with the egg yolks beaten in, and add the cloves, vanilla, and sugar. Stir continually with a wooden spoon until the mixture begins to thicken. Remove from the fire, add the almonds, and cool. When the mixture is quite cool, strain and add the aguardiente, brandy, or bourbon. Refrigerate twelve hours or several weeks before drinking. May be bottled after the twelve hours of refrigeration and kept indefinitely. Serve cold in small liqueur glasses.

MAKES 10 CUPS.

Sangría originated in Spain but it is popular throughout Mexico. There are many variations of sangría, but all contain dry red wine. Try this version for an accompaniment to a lovely luncheon.

Sangría

Sangría

2 cups club soda ·
1 ounce sugar ·
2 cups orange juice
(the juice of fresh
oranges is better) ·
2 tablespoons of
lemon juice ·
1 bottle (4/5 qt.)
dry red wine ·
crushed ice ·

Dissolve the sugar in the club soda; add the juices and the wine. May be served from a punch bowl with thin slices of oranges and lemons for garnish. Serve over crushed ice in punch cups or small glasses.

MAKES 16 SERVINGS OF 1/2 CUP EACH.

Garapiña

Fermented Pineapple Juice

In a large container put 12 quarts of water, three peeled and crushed pineapples, and 6 pounds of sugar. Stir until the sugar is completely dissolved.

Leave at room temperature for four days; then pour into bottles and seal so that the bottles are airtight. Will keep indefinitely as long as the seal is airtight. Chill before serving.

MAKES APPROXIMATELY 12 QUARTS.

Licor de Café

Coffee Liquer

Make a sugar syrup by combining two cups of granulated sugar and one cup of water in a pan. Stir over heat until the sugar is dissolved and the mixture is boiling. Allow to boil slowly for 8 minutes without stirring. The syrup should be rather thick. Add 1/2 cup of instant coffee and two tablespoons of vanilla; mix well and cool. Then add one bottle (4/5 quart) of vodka.

Pour into bottles or jars and cover tightly. It is not necessary to seal liqueurs. Place in a cool, dark place for three weeks; shake occasionally. Serve at room temperature.

MAKES APPROXIMATELY 1-1/2 QUARTS.

Licor de Naranja

Orange Liqueur

Make a sugar syrup by combining one cup of granulated sugar and one cup of water. Stir over heat until the sugar is dissolved. Add the grated rind of four large oranges and one tablespoon of vanilla. Boil slowly for 7 minutes without stirring. Cool.

Mix the orange sugar syrup with one bottle (4/5 quart) of brandy.

Pour into bottles or jars and cover tightly. Place in a cool, dark place for 3 or 4 weeks; shake occasionally. Serve at room temperature or over ice.

MAKES APPROXIMATELY 5 CUPS.

Licor de Fresa

Strawberry Liqueur

Mash one quart of strawberries. Dissolve one pound of sugar in three cups boiling water. Pour over the strawberries and press through a colander to extract juice.

Cover well, and when cool, add 2 cups of pure grain alcohol. (Pure grain alcohol is readily available in Mexico and can be purchased at liquor stores or some drug stores in the United States.) Leave at room temperature for two days; then strain again and pour into bottles. The mixture will keep in the refrigerator indefinitely, or you may serve it at room temperature immediately.

MAKES APPROXIMATELY 6—8 CUPS.

Licor Crema a la Vainilla

Vanilla Cream Liqueur

Chop two vanilla beans into small pieces and marinate in one quart of pure grain alcohol or vodka for one hour.

Make a syrup by boiling 4 cups of water and one pound of sugar for 5 minutes. Boil slowly and stir occasionally. Cool and add the alcohol and vanilla mixture. Pour into bottles (they do not need to be sealed) and place in a cool, dark place for three weeks; shake occasionally. Serve in small glasses at room temperature. Top each glass with a tablespoon of whipped cream.

MAKES APPROXIMATELY 2 QUARTS.

Crema de Fresas

Cream of Strawberries

2 quarts milk ·
4 cups sugar ·
1 teaspoon vanilla ·
6 egg yolks,
well-beaten ·
1 quart of
strawberries ·

Stir the sugar in the milk; add the vanilla and bring to a boil, stirring constantly. Remove from the fire; cool; then add the well-beaten egg yolks.

Wash strawberries well. Reserve a few of the whole strawberries for garnish. Press the remaining berries through a colander or sieve to extract their juice. Add the strained strawberries to the sugar and milk mixture. Chill the mixture in the refrigerator. Serve cold in cups. Top with whipped cream and a few strawberries cut in quarters.

MAKES 2-1/2 QUARTS (10 CUPS).

The word "atole" is a Mexican word which means a drink made of corn meal. The following "atole" drinks contain ingredients readily available in the United States: white flour may be substituted for the white corn meal if you so desire. Some stores now sell foil packets of instant Atole to which it is necessary only to add water or milk.

Atole de Fresa

Strawberry Drink

1-1/2 quarts fresh strawberries · 1/2 cup white corn meal or substitute 1/2 cup all-purpose wheat flour · 4 cups milk, scalded · 2 cups water · 1 cup sugar · 1 teaspoon vanilla · 1 cup light cream · few drops of red food coloring ·

Mash the well-washed strawberries and press through a colander or wet cloth to extract juice. Blend the white corn meal or flour with the water; add the scalded milk a little at a time, stirring continually. Put the mixture on the stove; gradually add the sugar, and continue stirring about 10 minutes. The mixture should be thick. Add the strawberry juice, vanilla, cream, and several drops of red food coloring. Heat to boiling, stirring continually. Serve hot in cups or mugs.

MAKES 2 QUARTS.

Atole de Leche

Milk Drink

2 cups water · 1/2 cup white corn meal or all-purpose wheat flour · 1-inch cinnamon stick · 4 cups milk · 1 cup sugar ·

Blend the corn meal or flour in the water; add the stick of cinnamon. Boil about 10 minutes, stirring from time to time. Then add the milk and sugar; bring to a second boil, stirring continually. Remove the cinnamon stick. Serve hot in cups or mugs.

MAKES 1-1/2 QUARTS (8 TO 10 SERVINGS).

18

Atole de Piña

Pineapple Drink

**1 small ripe
pineapple · 1/2 cup
white corn meal or
all-purpose wheat
flour · 8 cups of
milk or water ·
1 cup of sugar ·**

Peel the pineapple; chop and grind the pulp. Blend the corn meal or flour with the milk or water, adding the liquid gradually, while stirring. Add sugar. Cook until it begins to thicken but does not boil. Serve very hot in cups or mugs.

MAKES 8 CUPS.

Atole de Almendras

Almond Drink

**1/2 cup corn meal
or all-purpose
wheat flour · 2 cups
water · 2-inch
cinnamon stick ·
1 cup sugar ·
1/2 cup almonds,
blanched and
ground · 4 cups
milk ·**

Blend the corn meal or flour with the water, adding the water gradually, while stirring. Add the cinnamon stick and boil until the mixture thickens. Add sugar and milk; bring to a boil. Allow to cool about 15 minutes; add the blanched and ground almonds. Bring to a boil again; strain the almonds and cinnamon stick from the mixture. Serve hot in cups or mugs.

MAKES 6–8 CUPS.

Atole Blanco

White Corn Meal Drink

3/4 cup white corn meal or all-purpose wheat flour · 6 cups water · 2-inch cinnamon stick · 3/4 cup sugar ·

Blend the corn meal with the water, adding the water gradually, while stirring. Add the cinnamon stick and bring to a boil, stirring continually. When the mixture begins to thicken, add the sugar and boil another 5 minutes, stirring from time to time. Strain and serve hot in cups or mugs.

MAKES 6 CUPS OR 1-1/2 QUARTS.

Champurrado

Chocolate with Corn Meal

1 cup white corn meal · 1 cup water · 2-inch cinnamon stick · 6 cups milk · 1 cup sugar · 3 one-ounce squares of unsweetened chocolate ·

Blend the corn meal in one cup of water; add the cinnamon and bring to a boil. Remove from the heat.

In another pan, bring the milk, sugar, and chocolate to a boil. Be sure the chocolate has melted. Stir in the corn meal mixture. Remove the cinnamon stick and serve hot in cups.

SERVES 6–8 CUPS.

Chocolate en Agua

Chocolate in Water

6 ounces sweet chocolate · 4 cups water ·

Bring two cups of water to a boil and add the chocolate. Stir until the chocolate is melted; add the remaining water. Bring to a boil again; beat with an egg or wire beater until the mixture foams and serve hot in cups.

MAKES 4 CUPS (8 OUNCE SERVINGS).

Mexicans still use a beater called a "molinillo," which was designed by the ancient Mexican Indians. If you want to go native, you may purchase a molinillo in a number of shops in the United States. Refer to the ads in magazines or ask a teacher of Spanish about ordering one for you. Pour the chocolate mixture into a pitcher and beat with the molinillo until foamy.

Chocolate en Leche

Chocolate in Milk

6 ounces sweet chocolate · 4 cups milk ·

Bring the chocolate and milk to a boil, stirring constantly. Remove from the fire and allow it to settle. Repeat this process twice more. Beat until foamy with a conventional beater or with the "molinillo" until foamy and serve hot in cups.

MAKES 4 CUPS (8 OUNCE SERVINGS).

Atole de Guayaba

Guava Corn Meal Drink

1 cup white corn meal or all-purpose wheat flour · 1/2 cup water · 2-inch cinnamon stick · 2 cups sugar · 6 cups milk, scalded · 1 cup fresh guava, peeled and crushed ·

Blend the corn meal in the water; add the cinnamon stick and boil until the mixture begins to change color, stirring continually. Add the sugar, scalded milk, and guavas. Boil, stirring constantly, until the mixture begins to thicken. Strain and serve hot in cups or mugs.

SERVES 6 (8 OUNCE MUGS).

A favorite drink discovered in the Halls of Montezuma by the Spanish conquerors was chocolate. Even today, Mexican chocolate does not resemble the instant variety found on grocery shelves in the United States. However, these recipes do contain ingredients that can be purchased here.

Atole de Chocolate

Chocolate Atole

1/2 cup all-purpose wheat flour · 1 cup brown sugar · 3 cups milk · 3 cups water · 3 1-ounce squares unsweetened chocolate, grated · 2-inch cinnamon stick ·

Using 1/4 cup of the water, melt the grated chocolate in a double boiler until smooth; set aside. Place the flour in a large saucepan, and stir in remaining water. Add the cinnamon stick and cook over a low heat, stirring constantly, until the mixture thickens. Remove from heat, and add the sugar, milk, and melted chocolate. Return to heat, and bring to a simmer. Remove the cinnamon stick. Beat lightly and serve hot.

MAKES 7 CUPS.

Champurrado is a Mexican term for a chocolate drink made with atole. This term is not used in other Spanish-speaking countries.

Café con Leche

Coffee with Milk

Among the native Mexicans, coffee served with milk is very popular. Hot milk is served in one pitcher and hot coffee in another pitcher. The proportions are mixed equally in a cup, but for each cup of coffee, allow 4 tablespoons of ground coffee brewed in a coffee pot.

las sopas

3

soups

Soup is a very important and necessary element of the Mexican meal. It is generally the first course of the large meal of the day, which is served between 1:30 and 2:30 in the afternoon. These soups are deliciously different from any I have ever tasted in the United States. A number of them are filling enough to be main dishes.

Many of the recipes call for "caldo," which, in Spanish, means "broth." Broth is the water in which chicken, meats, fish, or vegetables have been cooked; the broth is often refrigerated or frozen for future use. Since many types of bouillon cubes or canned broths are readily available in the grocery stores here, I have substituted them when the recipe calls for "caldo."

Sopa de Aguacate

Avocado Soup

4 tablespoons butter or shortening · 2 tablespoons flour · 2 tablespoons chopped onion · 4 cups chicken broth · 3 to 5 medium-sized avocados, mashed · 1/2 cup sour cream · 2 tortillas · salt and pepper ·

Heat one tablespoon butter. or shortening; sauté onion about 2 minutes (do not brown). Gradually blend in the flour and brown. Add the chicken broth a little at a time, stirring continually; salt and pepper to taste. Simmer 15 minutes. Pour into soup tureen.

Top with peeled and mashed avocados mixed with sour cream; stir. Serve with tortillas cut into small squares and fried until golden brown in 3 tablespoons butter or shortening. Serve either hot or ice cold.

SERVES 6.

Sopa de Elote

Corn Soup

2 ounces butter · 1 medium-sized onion, diced · 6 tablespoons tomato sauce (2 tomatoes, peeled, seeded, and chopped, may be substituted for the sauce) · 8 cups chicken broth · 6 tender ears of corn · salt and pepper ·

Sauté the onion in the butter until soft; add the tomatoes or tomato sauce and the chicken broth; bring to a boil. Lower the fire to simmer.

Cut the kernels from the corn cobs. Put half of the corn in the broth; blend the other half in an electric blender for 30 seconds; then add this corn to the broth also. Salt and pepper to taste. Simmer 30 minutes and serve hot.

SERVES 8–10.

Sopa de Frijol

Bean Soup

3/4 cup dried red or kidney beans · 1 medium-sized onion, sliced · 1/2 cup tomato paste · 1/2 teaspoon oregano · 1/2 cup sharp cheddar cheese, grated · 4 tortillas · 4 tablespoons shortening or bacon fat · salt and pepper

Soak the well-washed beans overnight in 3 quarts (12 cups) of water. Cook the beans over low heat in the same water in which they were soaked with an onion and 1 tablespoon of shortening or bacon fat. Cover and cook over low heat for 1-1/2 hours or until the beans are soft. Purée the beans in a blender.

In a frying pan, melt a tablespoon of shortening or bacon fat; simmer the tomato paste about 5 minutes. Add the tomato mixture, the puréed beans, and the oregano to the broth. Salt and pepper to taste. Bring to a boil. Garnish each serving with grated cheese. Serve with tortillas cut into small squares and fried until golden brown in two tablespoons of shortening or bacon fat.

SERVES 6.

Sopa de Frijol Negro

Black Bean Soup

1 pound small black beans · 1 hambone · 1 onion, chopped · 2 teaspoons salt · 2 tablespoons lime juice · 2 sprigs parsley · 6 radishes, chopped ·

Black beans are not always easy to obtain, but they should be available in specialty shops. The dried red or kidney beans in the "Sopa de Frijol" recipe may be substituted for black beans.

Soak the beans overnight in 4 cups of water. Cook them over low heat in the same water in which they have been soaking. Bring to a boil; add the hambone, onion, and salt. Cover and cook gently until the beans are soft (about 5 hours if you are using black beans). Purée the beans in a blender. Return the purée to the soup pot; and add the lime juice; bringing to a boil. Serve hot, garnished with parsley and chopped raw radishes.

SERVES 6.

Sopa de Gallina

Chicken Soup

1 tender hen (3 to 4 pounds) · 2 tablespoons cooking oil · 3 large tomatoes, peeled and chopped · 1 medium-sized onion, chopped · 2 cloves of garlic, peeled and chopped · 1/2 cup dry sherry wine · 3/4 teaspoon salt ·

Cover the chicken with hot water (about 6 cups) and simmer, covered, until the chicken is tender—about one hour. Remove the meat from the bones and dice the chicken.

Fry the tomatoes, onion, and garlic in the cooking oil until the onions begin to turn brown. To this mixture add 2 cups of chicken stock, the chicken, the sherry, and salt. Bring to a boil and simmer 15 minutes.

SERVES 6.

Sopa Barata

Cheap Soup

3 tomatoes, peeled
and finely
chopped · 3 garlic
cloves, finely
chopped ·
1 medium-sized
onion, finely
chopped ·
1 teaspoon salt ·
1 sprig parsley,
finely chopped ·
2 egg yolks,
well-beaten · oil ·

Warm enough oil to cover the bottom of the pot and fry the tomatoes, garlic, onion, and parsley until the onions begin to brown. Add three cups of water; add salt. Boil for 30 minutes; strain.

When ready to serve, stir in the well-beaten egg yolks and serve hot.

SERVES 4.

Sopa de Ajo

Garlic Soup

3 cloves garlic,
finely chopped ·
2 slices white
bread, diced ·
1 tablespoon olive
oil or cooking oil ·
4 cups clear
chicken broth or
stock ·
3 tablespoons dry
white wine
(optional) ·
1 teaspoon salt ·

Heat enough oil to cover the bottom of the pot; add the garlic cloves and the diced bread; fry until the bread cubes are a golden brown. Remove from the pot; blend or pound this mixture to a paste.

Add the chicken broth, wine, salt, and the bread and garlic mixture to the pot. Cook over medium heat for 30 or 40 minutes. Put the soup mixture through a colander and serve the broth hot.

Garlic Soup may be served cold by chilling it in the refrigerator. Garnish with an ice cube in each plate.

SERVES 4.

Sopa de Calabaza

Squash Soup

4 medium sized zucchini squash · 4 tablespoons butter · 1 onion, finely chopped · 1 tablespoon flour · 2 cups milk · 1/2 cup light cream · 2 slices white bread, cut in small cubes · 1 tablespoon salt · 1/4 teaspoon black pepper ·

Wash the zucchini squash, remove ends, and cut each squash in half. Place the squash in a pan of boiling water to which 1 tablespoon of salt has been added. Cover and simmer about 10 minutes, or until the zucchini is tender. Drain, reserving 1 cup of water, and chop in small pieces.

Heat 2 tablespoons butter or margarine in a pan and fry onion until soft. Shake the flour and the cup of reserved water together in a jar, as this makes a much smoother blend. Add this mixture to the onion a little at a time, stirring continually until the mixture begins to boil. Add zucchini, milk, salt, and black pepper. Simmer about 15 minutes, stirring from time to time, and being careful that the mixture does not boil.

Before serving, fry the bread cubes in 2 tablespoons of butter until golden brown. Add the cream and the fried bread cubes to the soup. Serve hot.

SERVES 6.

Mexicans are not very fond of potatoes, so you will find very few of their recipes containing them. Instead, they prefer to eat their starch in the form of dry soups (Chapter 4). But here is a potato soup called "Snow Soup"—not only for its color but because of the "peaks" of egg whites used for garnish.

Sopa de Nieve

Snow Soup

4 medium-sized potatoes · 1 slice toasted white bread · 2 cups milk, scalded · 2 eggs · 1 tablespoon butter · 3/4 teaspoon salt · 3/4 teaspoon white pepper ·

Peel and slice the potatoes; put them in a pan with enough water to cover. Add the toasted bread, which has been diced. Boil until the potatoes are nearly tender.

Drain the liquid from the potatoes; add the scalded milk; and continue cooking until the potatoes are tender. Press them through a colander. Return the mixture to the soup pot, and add 2 egg yolks beaten together with 2 tablespoons of milk. Add salt, pepper, and butter. Heat, but do not boil.

Beat the egg whites until stiff. Before serving, spoon some of the egg white mixture on each serving to resemble peaks of snow.

SERVES 4.

Sopa de Crema de Chicharos

Cream of Pea Soup

1 cup of canned
English peas
(number 3 size) ·
4 small onions
sliced in ring form ·
2 tablespoons
butter or margarine
· 4 cups of broth
(vegetable, beef, or
chicken) · 1/2 cup
heavy cream ·
1/2 teaspoon salt ·

Warm the peas in their own liquid. Drain and mash half of this mixture. Fry the onion rings in the butter until they are soft but not brown. To the broth add the peas, onions, and salt; bring to a boil and remove from the fire. Stir in the cream and serve.

SERVES 6.

Sopa de Verduras

Vegetable Soup

2 onions, chopped ·
2 tablespoons
butter · 4 stalks
celery, chopped ·
3 ripe tomatoes,
peeled, chopped ·
4 tablespoons
rice · 6 beef
bouillon cubes ·
1 teaspoon salt ·
1/4 teaspoon black
pepper · 2 egg
yolks, well-beaten ·

Fry the onions in the butter until onion is soft; add celery and tomatoes; cook until the tomatoes are soft. Add six cups of water, then add the rice, bouillon cubes, salt, and pepper. Simmer 1 hour.

When ready to serve, stir in the egg yolks.

SERVES 6.

Sopa de Higados de Res

Beef Liver Soup

1/2 pound calves' liver ·
2 tablespoons butter ·
1/2 tablespoon parsley, finely chopped ·
1/2 teaspoon ground cinnamon ·
1/4 teaspoon ground nutmeg ·
1 pound (16 ounce can) tomatoes ·
6 cups strained beef stock ·
3/4 teaspoon salt ·

Heat the butter and sauté the liver slowly until tender. Cut the liver into pieces and purée it in an electric blender with 1 cup of the beef stock until smooth.

In the soup pot add the parsley, cinnamon, nutmeg, tomatoes, the rest of the beef stock, the puréed liver mixture, and salt; bring slowly to a boil. Boil 5 minutes and serve hot.

SERVES 6.

Sopa de Queso

Cheese Soup

2 cups cheddar cheese, grated ·
2 tablespoons flour ·
1/8 teaspoon cayenne pepper ·
6 cups clear beef broth ·
2 tablespoons butter ·
1 medium-sized onion, diced · 2 egg yolks, beaten ·
3/4 teaspoon salt ·
1/2 teaspoon paprika ·

Put the cheese, flour, cayenne pepper, nutmeg and 1 cup of the beef broth in a blender and blend until the mixture is smooth.

In the soup pot, melt the butter and fry the onion until soft but not brown. Add the rest of the beef broth, the cheese mixture, and salt. Simmer about 15 minutes; then slowly stir in the egg yolks. Serve hot; sprinkle each helping with a few grains of paprika.

SERVES 6.

Sopa de Arroz y Jitomate

Rice and Tomato Soup

1 large onion, finely chopped ·
3 tablespoons pure vegetable oil ·
2 cups (1-16 ounce can) tomatoes ·
2 cloves garlic, crushed · 4 cups water · 1 teaspoon salt · 1/8 teaspoon ground red pepper ·
1/2 cup tender grain enriched rice

Sauté the onion in the oil over medium heat until the onion is soft but not brown. Add the tomatoes and crushed garlic and simmer five minutes. Add water; season with salt and a pinch of red pepper. Simmer for 15 minutes more. Pass this mixture through a colander and return the liquid to the fire. Bring to a boil; add rice. Lower the fire and simmer for 15 minutes. Serve hot.

SERVES 4.

Sopa de Arroz con Ostiones

Rice Soup With Oysters

1/2 cup tender grain enriched rice ·
2 cloves garlic, crushed · 1 parsley stem, chopped ·
1 medium-sized onion, chopped finely ·
4 tablespoons butter · 1 pint oysters ·
3/4 teaspoon salt ·

Oysters are available in pint containers at the meat counters of many grocery stores or meat markets during the fall and winter months.

Melt the butter in a pan and fry the rice, garlic, parsley, and onion until the rice begins to brown. Drain the oysters, reserving the liquid in a measuring cup; add enough water to measure two cups and put in the pan. Simmer 15 minutes. Add the oysters and the salt. Simmer 15 minutes more, stirring from time to time. Serve hot.

SERVES 4.

Sopa de Tortilla

Omelet Soup

1 medium-sized zucchini squash · 1 medium-sized onion, finely chopped · 2 tablespoons butter · 2 tablespoons flour · 8 cups chicken stock or broth · 2 egg yolks, beaten · 1/2 cup light cream · 3/4 tablespoon salt · 1/4 teaspoon pepper ·

Cook the zucchini and onion in salted water until the squash is tender. Drain and chop very fine, or blend in a blender, as the Mexican cook would do.

Make a roux by melting two tablespoons of butter in the pan (do not use a butter substitute), and blending in two tablespoons of flour over low heat, stirring continually for about 3 minutes; then slowly stir in 1 cup of chicken broth, stirring until the mixture is thickened and smooth. I recommend a wooden spoon for this.

Slowly stir in the remaining broth, the squash and onion mixture, and salt and pepper. Simmer 30 minutes. Remove from the fire; beat the egg yolks into the cream and add to the soup. Serve immediately with your favorite crackers.

SERVES 8.

Sopa Poblana

Puebla-Style Soup

1 cup cooked pork meat · 2 tablespoons vegetable cooking oil · 1 medium onion, finely chopped · 2 ears corn · 3 small zucchini squash · 2 large green peppers · 8 cups broth (chicken broth is good) · 6 tablespoons tomato paste · 1 tablespoon salt · 1/2 teaspoon pepper · 2 ounces Monterey Jack cheese, grated · 2 avocados, peeled and chopped ·

Cut the pork in bite size pieces; fry in the oil. When it begins to brown, add the onion, the corn cut from the cob, the zucchini cut in small pieces, and the green pepper with seeds removed and cut in small pieces. Add the tomato paste and the broth; season with salt and pepper. Simmer 45 minutes or until the vegetables are tender.

May be strained and served as a broth, or served as a soup with the vegetables and meat left in the soup. In either case, just before serving garnish each serving with the chopped avocados and cheese.

SERVES 10.

Sopa de Fideos

Vermicelli Soup

1/2 cup vermicelli, broken in pieces · 2 tablespoons vegetable oil or olive oil · 1 small onion, sliced · 2 tablespoons tomato purée · 6 cups chicken broth or stock · 1 sprig parsley, chopped · 1 teaspoon salt · 1/4 teaspoon pepper · 1/4 cup parmesan cheese, grated ·

In a pan, fry the uncooked vermicelli in the oil until it turns a golden color. Set aside. Fry the onion in the same oil with the tomato purée until the mixture is dry. Slowly stir in the broth. Add the spaghetti and parsley, and season with salt and pepper. Simmer about 15 minutes until the vermicelli is tender. Serve hot, garnished with the cheese.

SERVES 6.

Sopa de Fideos con Leche

Vermicelli Soup with Milk

1 cup vermicelli, broken in pieces · 1 tablespoon salt · 4 cups milk ·

Cook the vermicelli according to the instructions on the package, but do **not** overcook. Drain and put aside.

Bring the milk to a boil, and season with salt. Add the vermicelli and simmer for 5 minutes. Take from the fire and let stand for 5 minutes before serving.

SERVES 4.

Sopa de Jaibas

Crab Soup

16 small hard-shell crabs, or 1 cup canned crab meat (8 ounces) · 1 cup tomatoes, peeled and chopped · 2 medium-sized potatoes, peeled and diced · 4 cloves garlic, crushed · 2 medium-sized onions, diced · 1 tablespoon flour · 3 tablespoons butter · 4 cups water · 1 tablespoon white vinegar · 1/4 teaspoon black pepper · 1 sprig parsley, chopped · 1 tablespoon salt ·

Fry the tomatoes, garlic, and onions in 1 tablespoon of butter until the onions are soft but not brown. Set aside. In another pan make a roux by melting 2 tablespoons of butter, and blending in 1 tablespoon of flour. Simmer, stirring continually about 2 minutes.

Slowly stir 4 cups of water, the crab meat, the fried tomato mixture, the potatoes cut into pieces, and the vinegar, salt, pepper, and parsley together. Simmer one hour until the potatoes and crab meat are tender.

SERVES 6.

38

Sopa de Almejas

Clam Soup

2 garlic cloves, pressed · 4 tablespoons olive oil, or vegetable oil · 2 large tomatoes, peeled and chopped · 1 large onion, diced · 2 dozen clams, boiled and chucked · 4 cups clam broth · 1 teaspoon salt · 1 teaspoon black ground pepper · 1 teaspoon paprika ·

Brown garlic in hot oil; add onions and brown lightly. Add tomatoes and fry slowly for 10 minutes.

Wash and scrub the clams; put them in a pan of boiling water. Boil for about 3 minutes until their shells open and the juice runs. Then take them from their shells and chop finely. Reserve the water in which they are boiled.

Measure 4 cups of clam broth water. Add garlic, onion, and tomato mixture; add salt, pepper, and paprika. Simmer 30 minutes.

SERVES 8.

Sopa de Camarones

Shrimp Soup

2 pounds fresh shrimp · 4 tablespoons butter · 1 tablespoon flour · 1 large onion, chopped finely · 2 garlic cloves, chopped finely · 1 cup soup stock · 1 teaspoon salt · 1/4 teaspoon pepper · 2 slices bread, cut into 1-inch squares and fried ·

Cook the shrimp in boiling salted water for 15 minutes. If you are using frozen shrimp, follow the directions on the package. Drain, peel, and cut each shrimp in thirds.

Melt the butter; stir in one tablespoon of flour, the onion, and the garlic; continue stirring until the flour begins to brown. Stir in the shrimp, broth, salt and pepper. Cook 30 minutes.

Fry the bread cubes in oil until a light brown color.

Garnish with bread cubes and serve hot.

SERVES 4.

Sopa de Ostiones

Oyster Soup

3 egg yolks ·
3 teaspoons flour ·
4 cups milk · 1 pint
oysters ·
3 tablespoons
butter ·
3/4 teaspoon salt ·
1/4 teaspoon
pepper ·
1/4 teaspoon
grated nutmeg ·

Add the egg yolks and the flour to the milk and beat well with a slotted spoon.

Drain oysters, reserving liquid. Pour the oyster liquid into the milk mixture. In a frying pan, melt the butter and simmer the oysters about 5 minutes. Add the oysters to the milk mixture; add salt and pepper. Heat over a low fire, but do not boil. Before serving, top with dash of nutmeg in the soup tureen or individual bowls.

SERVES 4.

Sopa de Tortuga

Turtle Soup

The green turtle for preparing true turtle soup is found in the warm water of the West Indies. However, the terrapin or snapping turtle is a freshwater variety found in streams in the United States. This is a less expensive item than imported turtle meat. Canned or frozen turtle meat is available in grocery stores, meat markets, or specialty stores; but if you are unable to find it in your area, substitute five pounds of veal meat with bones for the turtle meat for a delicious mock turtle soup. Sea turtle soup is a favorite in Baja California, Mexico.

1 pound turtle meat · 2 garlic cloves, chopped · 1 sprig parsley, chopped · 2 cups canned tomatoes · 2 tablespoons vegetable cooking oil · 1 cup dry sherry · cayenne pepper, a few grains · 1/4 teaspoon freshly ground black pepper · 3/4 teaspoon salt ·

Cook the turtle meat in enough water to cover until tender (about 2 hours). Remove from pan and cut in bite size pieces.

Heat the oil and fry the garlic, onion, parsley, and tomatoes until the onions are soft but not brown. Add this mixture and the turtle pieces to the turtle broth and simmer 30 minutes. Just before serving, stir in the sherry, cayenne pepper, black pepper, and salt.

SERVES 8.

Sopa de Pescado

Fish Soup

3 pounds fish heads · 4 cloves garlic · 1 medium-sized onion, chopped · 2 sprigs parsley, chopped · 3 cups of water · 2 tablespoons olive oil · salt to taste · 1 cup dry sherry wine · 8 pitted large ripe olives, sliced ·

Simmer the fish heads, garlic, onion, and parsley in a pan with 3 cups water for 10-15 minutes. Remove the fish heads, but return any edible meat to the broth.

Add the oil and salt to taste. Simmer another 15 minutes, stirring occasionally. Before serving add the wine and garnish each helping with the sliced olives.

SERVES 6–8.

Caldo Largo Alvaradeño

Long Alvaradeño Broth (Fish)

2 pounds white fish filets · 3 medium sized tomatoes, chopped · 2 medium-sized onions, diced · 2 cloves of garlic, crushed · 1/2 teaspoon leaf oregano · 3/4 teaspoon salt · 1/4 teaspoon ground black pepper · 4 cups water · 3 tablespoons vegetable oil · 2 slices white bread cut in 1 inch cubes ·

Put the fish, tomatoes, onions, garlic, oregano, salt, and pepper in the soup pot with 4 cups of water. Allow to simmer until the fish is tender.

Remove the fish from the liquid. Cut half of the fish in small pieces for garnish. Purée the remaining fish in the blender and return this portion to the pot. Continue to simmer.

Melt the oil and fry the bread cubes until they are a light brown. Set aside. Fry the remaining fish pieces in the same oil until they are a light brown.

Strain the soup mixture through a colander. Serve the remaining broth garnished with pieces of fried fish and bread.

SERVES 6.

Caldo sin Grasas

Broth Without Fat

soup bone · 1-1/2 pounds lean veal, cut in 1-inch pieces · 1 chicken breast · 1 medium onion, sliced · 2 carrots, sliced · 2 celery stalks, diced · 2 turnips, peeled and cut-up · 2 sprigs parsley, chopped · salt to taste ·

Put all of the ingredients in a pan with 6 cups of water and bring to boil. Lower the fire and simmer about 3 hours. Stir from time to time and add more salt if necessary.

Before serving, de-bone the chicken breast and slice. Remove the soup bone. For a true broth, strain through a colander and serve clear. The meats and vegetables may be served after the soup course.

SERVES 6.

Caldo de Pollo

Chicken Broth

1 tender 2-3 pound fryer chicken · 2 carrots, diced · 1 turnip, chopped · 1 celery stalk, chopped · 2 stems parsley, chopped · 1 lettuce leaf · 8 cups water salt to taste ·

Place the whole chicken, carrots, turnip, celery, parsley, and lettuce leaf in a pot with 8 cups of water. Cook over a medium fire for two hours. After one hour of cooking, salt to taste.

This broth is served clear. Remove the chicken, which may be served as a main dish as it is, or deboned and used for making chicken croquettes. (Recipe on page 175). Strain the broth and serve hot; serve the vegetables with the chicken course.

SERVES 6–8.

Caldo de Frijoles

Bean Broth

1 pound red beans · 1 large tomato, peeled and chopped · 1 small onion, diced · 2 tablespoons vegetable oil · 1/2 teaspoon ground coriander · 1 tablespoon salt or salt to taste · 1/2 cup grated cheddar cheese ·

Soak the beans overnight until they are soft.

Fry the onion and tomato in the vegetable oil until the onion is soft.

Measure the water in which the beans have soaked and add enough water to measure 7 cups. Simmer the bean mixture with the tomato, onion, coriander, and salt for 12–15 hours.

To serve as a broth, strain and serve hot. Serve the beans as a side dish, or leave all of the ingredients in the pot and serve as a soup. Garnish either the broth or the soup with cheese.

SERVES 6.

Caldo "Pronto Hecho"

"Fast Made" Broth

2 pounds lean stew meat · 7 cups water · 2 carrots, cut in thirds · 2 turnips, cut in fourths · 1 medium-sized onion, chopped · 2 celery stalks, chopped · salt to taste ·

Put the cut-up pieces of beef in a pot with the water and bring to a boil. Turn down the fire and simmer for 30 minutes.

Add the carrots, turnips, onions, and celery. Salt to taste and simmer another 30 minutes, or until the vegetables are tender. Strain the broth and serve hot. Put the meat and vegetables on a platter and serve as the main dish.

SERVES 6.

44

sopas secas

4

dry soups

Dry soups, or "sopas secas," which normally follow the soup course, are very popular in Mexico. In fact, the first course of soup generally is called "caldo" (broth), while the second, which we can prepare for the main course, is called "sopa" (soup). But no matter what the name, the basic ingredients are the same as those in the "wet" soups; the cooking method simply uses less liquid, and the dish is cooked until dry.

Arroz a la mejicana

Mexican-style Rice

1 cup enriched rice · 3 tablespoons vegetable oil · 2 cups water · 1 beef bouillon cube · 1/2 cup canned English peas · 6 tablespoons tomato purée · 3/4 teaspoon salt · 1/2 teaspoon onion juice · 2 chorizo sausages, or 8 link pork sausages · 2 hard-boiled eggs, sliced length-wise · 1 sprig chopped parsley · 2 ripe avocados, peeled and cut in strips ·

Fry the rice in the oil until the rice is a golden brown; drain. In a two-quart saucepan, warm the water and melt the bouillon cube; add peas, tomato purée, salt, onion juice, and rice; mix well; cover with a lid and simmer 14 minutes until the rice is dry.

Fry the sausages in a frying pan until well done; then slice in one inch pieces. Prepare the eggs and the avocados.

Place the rice in a serving dish, and garnish with the sausages, eggs, parsley, and avocados.

SERVES 6–8.

Arroz Verde

Green Rice

1 cup enriched rice, uncooked · 1/2 cup vegetable or olive oil · 3 medium-sized bell peppers, chopped · 1 medium-sized onion, chopped · 1 clove garlic, minced · 2 cups chicken broth · 1/4 teaspoon salt · 1 tablespoon butter · 1/4 cup parmesan cheese, grated ·

Soak rice for 15 minutes in warm water; drain. Sauté rice in the oil, but remove it from the pan before it browns. Sauté the peppers, onion, and garlic in a little oil until the onion browns. Return the rice to the pan; add the broth and salt. Simmer about 15 minutes until the rice is smooth and dry. Melt the butter in the mixture.

Garnish with the cheese and serve immediately.

SERVES 6.

Arroz con Ostiones

Rice with Oysters

1 cup enriched white rice, uncooked · 1/2 cup vegetable oil · 1 clove garlic, minced · 1 medium-sized onion, chopped · 1/3 cup fresh parsley, chopped · 1 pint oysters · 1/4 teaspoon salt · 1 cup water or vegetable stock ·

Soak the rice for 15 minutes in warm water; drain. Sauté rice in oil until golden brown. Add garlic, onion, and parsley. Sauté 3 more minutes; then drain off fat. Add the liquid from the oysters and the salt; simmer 15 minutes. Add the oysters and water or stock. Continue simmering until the rice is nearly dry and serve immediately.

SERVES 6.

47

Arroz con Pescado

Rice with Fish

2 pounds cod or haddock fillets · 1/2 cup vegetable or olive oil · 3 garlic cloves, chopped · 1 cup enriched rice, uncooked · 1 onion, chopped · 1 number 3 can stewed tomatoes · 2 cups water · salt to taste ·

Fry the whole fish fillets in oil until light brown; drain on a paper towel. Sauté the garlic in the same oil. Remove; then sauté the rice until a golden brown. Add chopped onion and tomatoes to rice; sauté until the onion is soft. Return the garlic to the pan. Add 2 cups of water and salt to taste. Bring to a boil and add fish. Lower fire to simmer and cook 15 minutes until the rice is dry and tender.

SERVES 6.

Arroz Blanco

White Rice

6 medium-sized bell pepper cases · 1/2 cup vegetable or olive oil · 1 cup white enriched rice, uncooked · 1/2 cup onions, chopped · 1 cup water or chicken stock · 1 cup milk · 1/2 teaspoon salt · 1/2 cup canned English peas, drained · 1/2 cup sharp cheese, grated ·

Cut the tops from the green peppers and remove seeds. Blanch by putting them in hot water for 5 minutes. Set aside.

Prepare the filling by heating the oil and sautéeing the rice and onions. Remove from the heat before the rice browns. Drain off oil. Add water or stock and cook over low heat until the liquid is absorbed. Add milk and salt; cook until the mixture is nearly dry. Stir in drained peas and continue cooking until the rice is dry.

Fill the pepper cases. Cover tops with grated cheese, and brown briefly under a broiler.

SERVES 6.

Arroz con Camarones

Rice with Shrimp

4 tablespoons vegetable oil · 1 cup enriched rice, uncooked · 2 large ripe red tomatoes, sliced · 3 garlic cloves, chopped · 1 pound fresh or frozen shrimp (cooked and shells removed) · salt to taste ·

In a frying pan, melt the oil and add the rice, tomatoes, and garlic. Sauté until the rice begins to brown. Add two cups of water, the cleaned shrimp, and salt to taste. Cover and simmer 15 minutes. When the rice is tender, serve hot.

SERVES 6–8.

Sopa Seca de Tortilla

Dry Tortilla Soup

6 tortillas, cut into strips (you may use frozen tortillas) · 4 tablespoons vegetable oil · 1 medium-sized onion, chopped · 1 garlic clove, minced · 1/4 cup tomato sauce · 1 tablespoon parsley flakes · 1 teaspoon chili powder · 1 tablespoon salt · 1/4 tablespoon pepper · 3 tablespoons butter · 1/4 cup grated parmesan cheese ·

Heat the oil, and fry the tortilla strips in the oil until crisp; drain on paper towels. In the same oil, sauté the onion and garlic until soft. Add the tomato sauce, parsley, chili powder, salt, and pepper. Bring to a boil.

Grease a casserole dish with butter. Put in a layer of fried tortilla strips; top with a layer of the sauce. Continue the layers until the sauce is consumed. Dot with any remaining butter and add the cheese. Bake in a moderate oven (350°) for fifteen minutes until the mixture is dry.

SERVES 4.

Tallarines con Chorizo

Noodles with Sausage

1 cup (8 ounces) egg noodles ·
2 quarts water ·
6 whole black peppercorns · 2 bay leaves ·
1/4 teaspoon thyme ·
1/2 teaspoon salt ·
2 tablespoons vegetable or olive oil · 2 chorizo sausages, or 12 small link sausages ·
1 medium-sized onion, chopped ·
2 garlic cloves, chopped ·
1 teaspoon parsley, chopped ·
1-1/2 cups tomato sauce, canned ·
1-1/4 cups cheddar cheese, grated ·

Cook the noodles, peppercorns, bay leaves, thyme, and salt in 2 quarts of boiling water. Boil for 10 minutes. Drain and set aside.

Fry the sausages in the oil about 15 minutes, or until they are cooked thoroughly. Drain on a paper towel. In the same pan, sauté onion, garlic, and parsley until the onion is soft. Stir in the tomato sauce.

Preheat oven to 350°. Place in a greased 2-quart ovenproof casserole dish in layers: noodles, (from which the whole peppercorns and bay leaf have been removed), sausages, (cut in small pieces), and the tomato mixture. Continue the layers, using all of the ingredients. Bake for 30 minutes, or until the tomato mixture begins to bubble. Top with the cheese; bake a few more minutes until the cheese melts.

SERVES 6.

Macarrones con Chorizo

Macaroni with Sausage

2 cups elbow macaroni · 2 quarts water · 1 pound chorizo or 1 pound ground pork sausage · 1 tablespoon bacon fat or oil · 1/2 cup onion, chopped · 3 cups tomato sauce, canned · 1 tablespoon ground coriander · salt and pepper to taste · 1/2 cup cheddar cheese, grated ·

Cook the macaroni in the water wtih 2 teaspoons salt until tender—about 10 minutes. Drain.

If you are using chorizo, remove the casings first. Fry the sausage in the fat about 15 minutes or until cooked thoroughly. Stir occasionally, breaking up any large pieces of sausage. Remove from the fire. In the grease remaining in the pan, sauté the onion until tender. Drain off any excess grease. Heat the onion with tomato sauce, coriander, and salt and pepper to taste.

Preheat the oven to 325°. Put in a greased 2-quart casserole dish in layers: macaroni, sausage, and the tomato mixture. Continue the layers, using all the ingredients. Bake 30 minutes or until the tomato mixture begins to bubble. Sprinkle the cheese on top and bake a few more minutes until the cheese melts.

SERVES 6–8.

Macarrones a la mejicana

Mexican-style Macaroni

1/2 pound large tube-shaped macaroni · 8 cups water · 3 tablespoons butter · 1 medium onion, chopped · 4 red or green small chiles or substitute 4 canned jalapeño peppers with seeds removed · 1 cup light cream · 6 ounces Monterey Jack cheese shredded · salt and pepper to taste ·

Boil the macaroni for 8 minutes in the water, to which 1 teaspoon of salt has been added. Drain and set aside.

Melt 2 tablespoons of butter in a pan, and sauté the onion until soft. Preheat oven to 350°. In a greased 2-quart casserole dish, arrange in layers: macaroni, onion, and chiles. Add salt, pepper, and light cream. Top with cheese. Bake for 30 minutes.

SERVES 6.

Sopa de Fideo y Garbanzos

Vermicelli and Chick Pea Soup

1 cup chick peas, canned · 2 tablespoons vegetable or olive oil · 1 medium-sized onion, chopped · 3 garlic cloves, minced · 1 large white potato, chopped · 2 cups water · 4 ounces vermicelli · 1/4 teaspoon salt · 1/8 teaspoon pepper ·

Fresh chick peas, which are available in this country, do not have the same flavor as those in Mexico. Therefore it is better to use the canned variety. Put the canned chick peas in a pan and heat. Drain and mash.

In the oil, sauté the onion, garlic, and potato for 10 minutes.

In the large pan with 2 cups water, add the chick peas, fried onion, garlic, potatoes, vermicelli, salt, and pepper. Simmer slowly about 12 minutes or until the vermicelli is tender. Serve immediately.

SERVES 6.

cacerolas y platos con arroz

casseroles and rice dishes

Any of the following recipes may be served as the second course of the "comida" as a substitute for a dry soup. In the United States, try them as the main course.

Macarrones al Graten

Macaroni with Cheese

2 cups macaroni ·
8 cups water ·
2 teaspoons salt ·
1/2 cup rich milk or
light cream ·
1/2 cup cheddar
cheese, grated ·
2 tablespoons
bread crumbs ·

Add the macaroni slowly to the boiling water seasoned with salt. Cook 10 minutes. Drain. Put in a buttered 2-quart casserole dish. Pour the milk or cream over the macaroni. Top with the cheese and bread crumbs. Bake in a preheated oven at 325° for about twenty-five minutes.

SERVES 6.

Macarrones al Natural

Natural Macaroni

2 cups elbow
macaroni · 8 cups
water · 3 medium
onions, chopped ·
3 tablespoons
vegetable or olive
oil · 1 teaspoon
salt ·

Slowly add the macaroni to the boiling water seasoned with salt, and boil 12 minutes. (The packaged macaroni will have directions for cooking.) Drain.

While the macaroni is cooking, heat the oil in a pan and sauté the onions until brown. Add the onions to the macaroni, season with a teaspoon of salt, and serve.

SERVES 6.

Macarrones con Coliflor

Macaroni with Cauliflower

2 cups macaroni ·
1 medium-sized
head of cauliflower
· 2 tablespoons
butter ·
2 tablespoons flour
· 1 cup milk ·
1 teaspoon salt ·
1/8 teaspoon
nutmeg · 1/2 cup
mild cheddar
cheese, grated ·
1 tablespoon
butter ·

Cook the macaroni in salted water according to the directions on the package. Drain and set aside.

Cut off the tough end of the cauliflower stem. Break the cauliflower into florets, and put them in a pan of boiling water (just enough to cover) seasoned with salt. Reduce heat to simmer. Cook about 12 minutes or until tender. Drain and set aside.

Make a roux by melting two tablespoons butter in a pan and blending in the flour over very low heat for 2 minutes. Gradually stir in the milk with a wooden spoon, if possible. Stir continually until thick and smooth. Add 1 teaspoon of salt and a pinch of nutmeg to milk mixture.

Preheat oven to 400°. In a buttered 2-quart casserole dish, put the macaroni; then add the cauliflower and the sauce. Top with cheese and dot with butter. Bake 10 minutes and serve very hot.

SERVES 6–8.

Macarrones con Ostiones

Macaroni with Oysters

2 cups elbow macaroni · 1 pint oysters · 1 teaspoon salt · 1/8 teaspoon ground black pepper · 1/2 cup light cream · 1/4 cup bread crumbs · a pinch of paprika · 4 tablespoons butter ·

Cook the macaroni in boiling salt water according to the directions on the package. Drain and set aside.

Cook the oysters in their own liquid over a low fire about five minutes or until the edges of the oysters begin to curl.

Preheat oven to 350°. In a buttered 2-quart casserole dish, mix the macaroni, oysters, and their liquid together. Stir in salt, pepper, and cream. Top with bread crumbs and a pinch of paprika. Dot with butter. Bake in the oven for fifteen minutes.

SERVES 6–8.

Macarrones Encebollados

Macaroni in Onion Sauce

3 medium-sized onions, chopped · 1/2 cup water · 2 cups elbow macaroni · white cream sauce (butter, flour, milk) · 1/8 teaspoon nutmeg · 1/2 teaspoon salt · 1 medium-sized eggplant peeled and cut crosswise into slices 1/2 inch thick · 2 tablespoons butter · 1-16 ounce can tomato sauce · salt and pepper to taste · 1/2 cup mild cheddar cheese, grated ·

White Cream Sauce:

Melt 2 tablespoons butter (do not use a substitute) in a pan. Blend in two tablespoons flour, stirring with a wooden spoon. Slowly add 1 cup of milk; stir continually until thick and smooth.

Boil the onions in 1/4 cup water over high flame for 5 minutes. Rinse with cold water and drain. Return to the fire with 1/4 cup water. Simmer the onions until soupy. Set aside.

Meanwhile, boil the macaroni in salted water according to the directions on the package. Drain when tender. Mix the macaroni with the white cream sauce, nutmeg, and salt.

Fry the eggplant slices in butter about 3 minutes. They do not need to be tender. Drain on a paper towel.

Extract all the liquid from the onions; mix this liquid with the tomato sauce, and add salt and pepper to taste.

Preheat oven to 350°. In a buttered 2-quart casserole dish, place in layers: 1 cup of tomato-onion sauce, 1 cup macaroni, a layer of eggplant. Top with any remaining tomato-onion sauce. Heat from 20–30 minutes. Five minutes before removing from the oven, top with grated cheese.

SERVES 6–8.

Tallarines con Queso y Jamón

Noodles with Cheese and Ham

2 cups egg noodles · 3 quarts water · 1 tablespoon salt · 1 cup cooked ham, diced · 1/8 teaspoon pepper · 1/4 cup whole milk · 1/4 cup sharp cheddar cheese, grated · 2 tablespoons butter ·

Put egg noodles into 3 quarts of rapidly boiling water with 1 tablespoon of salt. Cook uncovered, stirring occasionally, 7 to 10 minutes or until tender. Drain; rinse with warm water.

Preheat oven to 325°. In a buttered 2-quart casserole dish, mix the noodles and ham. Add the pepper and milk. Top with the cheese and dot with butter. Bake in the oven for ten minutes and serve hot.

SERVES 6–8.

Tallarines Económicos

Economical Noodles

2 cups egg noodles · 3 quarts water · 1 tablespoon salt · 1 medium-sized onion, chopped · 2 tablespoons vegetable or olive oil · 1 pound (16 ounce can) tomatoes · 1/2 tablespoon salt · 1 cup lean cooked pork, diced · 1/4 cup sharp cheddar cheese, grated ·

Put egg noodles into 3 quarts of rapidly boiling water with 1 tablespoon salt. Cook uncovered, stirring occasionally, 7 to 10 minutes or until tender. Drain; rinse with warm water.

Sauté the onion in oil until brown. Add the tomatoes, salt, and pork. Simmer for 5 minutes.

Preheat oven to 350°. In a buttered 2-quart casserole dish mix the noodles and pork mixture. Top with the grated cheese. Bake in the oven until the cheese melts—about 5 to 7 minutes. Serve hot.

SERVES 6–8.

Frijoles con Puerco

Beans with Pork

1 cup small red beans · 1 quart water · 2 tablespoons vegetable or olive oil · 4 garlic cloves, chopped · 1 small onion, chopped · 2 chili verdes (use canned green chili peppers) · 1 cup cooked pork, diced · 3/4 teaspoon salt · 1/4 cup mild cheddar cheese, grated ·

Soak beans overnight and cook, covered, in one quart of water until very tender (2-1/2 to 3 hours). Drain, but reserve 1 cup of the liquid.

Sauté the garlic, onion, and chili peppers in the oil until the onion is soft.

Preheat oven to 400°. In a buttered 2-quart casserole dish, mix the drained beans with the cup of reserved liquid, the onion mixture, the pork, and salt. Top with grated cheese and bake 5 minutes.

SERVES 6.

Budín de Calabacitas

Zucchini Pudding

The Spanish word "budín," which means pudding, is rather misleading here, for this is a zucchini squash casserole.

6 medium-sized zucchini · 6 medium cut pork chops · 1/4 cup vegetable or olive oil · 1 large onion, chopped · 2 garlic cloves, chopped · 1 can (16 ounces) tomatoes · 1 small can (8-1/4 ounces) whole kernel corn (drained) · 1/2 teaspoon salt · 1/4 teaspoon pepper · 1/2 cup medium cheddar cheese, grated ·

Wash zucchini and dice. Fry the pork chops in a frying pan with enough oil to keep from sticking. Set aside. In another pan, sauté the onions and garlic in 1/4 cup of oil until the onions are soft.

Preheat oven to 325°. In a buttered 2-quart casserole dish, add the zucchini, onion, garlic, canned tomatoes with their liquid, corn, salt, and pepper. Bake for 35 minutes, or until zucchini is tender; top with grated cheese and bake another 5 minutes.

SERVES 6.

Arroz con Jaibas

Rice with Crabs

3 tablespoons butter · 3 garlic cloves, chopped · 1 large onion, chopped · 1 cup uncooked rice · 4 tomatoes, peeled and chopped · 2 cups water · 2 cups canned, flaked crab meat · mint leaves ·

Saute the garlic and onion in the butter until the onion begins to brown. Add the rice; stir until brown. Add the tomatoes and enough water to cover (about 2 cups). Cook over a very low fire, stirring from time to time, until the rice is tender. Put in the crab meat and heat thoroughly.

Serve hot. In Mexico this dish is garnished with fresh mint leaves. If you have any, go native and try it.

SERVES 6.

Arroz a la Catalana

Catalan-Style Rice

1 pound link sausages · 1 medium-sized onion, chopped · 2 garlic cloves, chopped · 2 tablespoons butter · 1 cup uncooked rice · 1 teaspoon parsley · 1 teaspoon salt · 1/4 teaspoon pepper · 3 large tomatoes, peeled and chopped · 3 cubes bouillon · 2 cups water · 1 cup cooked ham, diced ·

Fry the sausages in a pan until they brown. Set aside. Add butter to the frying pan; brown the onion and garlic. Add the rice and stir for several minutes. Stir in the parsley, salt, pepper, and tomatoes. Dissolve the bouillon cubes in 2 cups of water, and add to the mixture.

When the mixture boils, place it in a 2-quart buttered casserole dish. Mix in the cooked ham, and top the dish with with link sausages. Bake in the lower part of the oven at 350° for 30 to 40 minutes.

SERVES 6.

Arroz Tropical

Tropical Rice

1 cup uncooked rice · 2 cups chicken broth or stock · 3 whole cloves · 1/4 cup butter · 4 ounce can grated coconut ·

Bring the chicken broth to a boil and add the rice and cloves. Simmer for 10 minutes. Remove the cloves. Add butter and coconut; cook 5 more minutes until the rice is tender.

SERVES 4.

Arroz en Tomatada

Rice with Fried Tomatoes

2 cups uncooked rice · 4 cups chicken broth or stock · 4 medium-sized tomatoes, peeled and sliced · 1/4 cup vegetable or olive oil · 1/2 teaspoon salt · 1/8 teaspoon black pepper ·

Bring the broth or stock to a boil. Add the rice and simmer 15 minutes.

While the rice is cooking, heat the oil and pan fry the tomato slices. Drain them on a paper towel.

Add salt and pepper to the rice. Serve on a large platter and top with fried tomatoes.

SERVES 6–8.

las salsas

6

sauces

Most Mexican dishes are not "picante," which means they are not seasoned hot. However, sauces in Mexican cooking or as side dishes are essential; and their use dates back to before the arrival of the Spaniards. Some of these recipes are for sauces seasoned with hot peppers, but they are served on the table as side dishes.

Salsa mejicana

Mexican Sauce

4 medium tomatoes, peeled and chopped fine · 1/2 cup onions, chopped fine · 1/2 cup celery, chopped fine · 1/4 cup green pepper, chopped fine · 1/4 cup olive oil · 1 teaspoon mustard seed · 3 canned green or red chilies, chopped · 2 tablespoons red wine vinegar · 1 teaspoon ground coriander · salt and pepper to taste ·

Here is an excellent basic recipe for a sauce to serve as a side dish with meats, eggs, vegetables, tacos, enchiladas, or tamales. For variety, add a couple of tablespoons of this sauce to soups.

There are many varieties of chilies grown in Mexico and also in this country. For a mild sauce use green chilies, but if you like a "picante" sauce, use Jalapeño chilies.

Combine all of the ingredients and mix well. Place the sauce in covered jars and refrigerate at least 8 hours before serving. Shake occasionally and serve cold. Will keep indefinitely in the refrigerator.

MAKES 2 PINTS OF SAUCE.

Salsa de Chile y Jitomate

Chili-Tomato Sauce

1 medium onion,
minced ·
2 tablespoons salad
oil · 3-1/2 cups
tomato purée ·
2 garlic cloves,
minced ·
4 tablespoons chili
powder ·
1/2 teaspoon
ground cumin seed
· 1/4 teaspoon
dried oregano ·
1 teaspoon salt ·

Sauté the onion in salad oil until it softens. Add the tomato purée and the garlic. Gradually add chili powder, cumin seed, oregano, and salt. Cover and simmer at least 30 minutes, stirring frequently. Strain through a sieve. Excellent for enchiladas.

MAKES ABOUT 4 CUPS OF SAUCE.

Salsa de Jitomate

Mexican Tomato Sauce

2 large ripe
tomatoes, peeled
and chopped ·
1 large onion, diced
· 1 tablespoon
ground coriander ·
2 tablespoons olive
oil · 2 serrano
chilies, chopped ·
salt and pepper to
taste ·

Combine the tomatoes, onion, coriander, and olive oil. Unless you have made a recent trip to Mexico or live in an area where serrano chilies are available, substitute any variety of small red or green hot chili. Add the chilies to the tomato mixture, and be sure to include the seeds. These make the sauce "picante." Salt and pepper to taste and refrigerate 8 hours before serving. Serve cold. Serve as a side dish for meats, eggs, or other foods for which you may prefer hot sauce.

MAKES 2 CUPS OF SAUCE.

Salsa de Tomate

Tomato Sauce

3 large ripe tomatoes, peeled and sliced · 1 small bay leaf · 1/2 teaspoon thyme · 4 garlic cloves, minced · salt and pepper to taste ·

Sauté tomatoes, bay leaf, thyme, garlic cloves, salt, and pepper in a pan until the tomatoes are soft. Pass the mixture through a colander, squeezing with force in order to extract all the sauce. This sauce is very rich, but it is not seasoned hot like the "Mexican Tomato Sauce" recipe. It is used to season pastas, and to garnish fish, meat, poultry, or eggs.

MAKES 2 CUPS OF SAUCE.

Salsa de Tomato Verde

Green Tomato Sauce

20 small green tomatoes, peeled and sliced · 3 mountain chiles, chopped · 1 onion, chopped · 2 garlic cloves, minced · 1/4 cup water · 1/4 teaspoon coriander · 1/4 teaspoon salt ·

Cook the tomatoes, onion, and garlic with the chiles in a little water until the tomatoes are soft. If necessary, substitute any variety of small red hot pepper for the mountain chiles.

Put this mixture in the blender with the coriander and salt. Blend thoroughly.

In Mexico, a sauce like "Tomato Verde" is always served on the table as a side dish. It can be used in soup; on fish, meat, or eggs; or as a sauce for tortillas. The hotter it is, the better.

MAKES 4 CUPS OF SAUCE.

Salsa Cuquina para Carnes Frias

Cuquina-Style Sauce for Cold Cuts

1 can (16 ounces)
canned tomatoes ·
1 large onion,
chopped ·
2 jalapeño chiles ·
1 medium-sized
tomato, peeled and
chopped fine ·
2 tablespoons
vinegar ·
3 tablespoons dried
oregano ·
1/2 teaspoon salt ·
1 tablespoon sugar
· 1/4 teaspoon
black ground
pepper ·

Blend the canned tomatoes, onion, and chiles in an electric blender. To this mixture, add the raw tomato, vinegar, oregano, and salt. Set aside for one or two hours at room temperature. Then add sugar and pepper. Will keep indefinitely in the refrigerator. Delicious served as a side dish with cold cuts of meat.

MAKES 2–3 CUPS OF SAUCE.

No Mexican cookbook is complete without including "Salsa Borracha" or "Drunken Sauce," although the term is misleading. If you are going, or if you have a friend who is going south of the border, bring back some pulque. It can be purchased on nearly any street corner.

Salsa Borracha

Drunken Sauce

8 serrano chiles (or substitute small green hot peppers) chopped · 2 cloves garlic, diced · 2 medium-sized onions, chopped · 2 tablespoons olive oil · 2 cups pulque or dry red wine · 1/4 cup sharp cheddar cheese, grated ·

Sauté chiles, garlic, and onion in the oil over a low fire until the onion is soft. Marinate this mixture in the pulque or wine for one hour at room temperature.

Drain the liquid and blend the chile mixture with the cheese added in the blender. Then mix with the pulque or wine. If placed in covered jars, the sauce will keep indefinitely in the refrigerator. Serve with any type of roast meat.

MAKES 2-1/2 CUPS OR ABOUT 24 SERVINGS.

Salsa española

Spanish Sauce

2 tablespoons olive oil · 1/2 cup onion, finely chopped · 2 tablespoons green pepper, chopped · 1 garlic clove, chopped · 2 cups canned tomatoes · 6 whole cloves · 1/4 teaspoon celery seed · 1 tablespoon sugar · 1 teaspoon salt · 1/4 teaspoon black pepper ·

Melt oil in frying pan; add onion, green pepper, garlic, and tomatoes. Sauté 10 minutes.

Add cloves, celery seed, sugar, salt, and pepper; and simmer for one hour. Stir occasionally to keep from sticking. Mixture should be thick. Serve as a side dish for any type of meat.

MAKES 2 CUPS.

Ajoaceite

Garlic Sauce

6 cloves garlic, chopped · 1/2 teaspoon salt · 1 egg yolk · 1/4 cup melted butter ·

This is the Mexican version of garlic butter. Put all of the ingredients in an electric blender and blend for 5 minutes, or until smooth. Serve with steak or use to make garlic bread.

MAKES 1/2 CUP.

Salsa de Mantequilla

Butter Sauce

8 tablespoons butter ·
1/4 teaspoon seasoned salt ·

Melt the butter with the salt in a pan without its boiling or becoming dark. Serve in a warmed bowl. Excellent with fish and vegetable dishes.

MAKES 1 CUP.

Salsa Real

Royal Sauce

4 cups chicken broth or stock ·
3 tablespoons butter ·
1 tablespoon flour ·
2 tablespoons lemon juice ·
1/2 teaspoon salt ·
1/8 teaspoon pepper ·

Shake the flour in a jar with 1/2 cup of broth. Melt the butter over low heat; slowly add the flour mixture and the rest of the chicken broth, stirring continually for 10 minutes. Add the lemon juice, salt, and pepper. Stir continually for 5 more minutes.

Serve as a side dish for fried, broiled, or baked chicken.

MAKES 3 CUPS.

Salsa Mahonesa

Mayonnaise Sauce

2 egg yolks ·
1/2 teaspoon salt ·
1 teaspoon sugar ·
4 tablespoons vinegar · 2 cups olive oil ·

Beat the eggs with an egg beater until thick; add salt, sugar, and 2 tablespoons (half) of the vinegar.

Continue to beat the egg mixture while adding the oil drop by drop, at first, gradually increasing the oil until the sauce is thick and shiny. Slowly add the remaining vinegar; beat well. Refrigerate before serving.

MAKES 2 CUPS.

70

Salsa Béchamel

Béchamel-Style Sauce

3 tablespoons butter · 2 tablespoons flour · a few grains of nutmeg · 1 teaspoon salt · 1 cup milk · 1 cup light cream · a few grains of cayenne · 1/4 teaspoon pepper ·

Here is the Mexican version of Béchamel sauce.

Melt butter over low heat; stir in the flour, nutmeg, salt, and pepper until well blended. Remove from the heat to avoid lumping and gradually stir in the milk and cream. Return to the heat, stirring constantly, until thick and smooth. Add a dash of cayenne. Serve immediately, or, if it is necessary to keep this sauce a while before serving, put a cover on the pan and place it over hot water, or use a double boiler.

Serve as a side dish with fried chicken or serve over baked chicken, fish, or vegetables.

MAKES 2 CUPS.

Salsa Blanca

White Sauce

4 tablespoons butter · 4 tablespoons flour · 1 teaspoon salt · 1/4 teaspoon pepper · 2 cups milk · 1 egg yolk, beaten ·

Melt butter over low heat; add flour, salt, and pepper. Stir until well blended. Remove from the heat and gradually stir in the milk, or heat the milk first, and it can be added to the mixture over low heat. Either method should prevent lumping.

Continue cooking over low heat, stirring continually, until smooth and thick.

Use this sauce with boiled potatoes, fish, or with any of the recipes in this book requiring white sauce.

MAKES 2 CUPS.

Salsa de Perejil y Almendras

Parsley and Almond Sauce

**1-1/2 cups parsley, well chopped ·
1 cup water ·
1/4 cup almonds, blanched ·
3 tablespoons white vinegar ·
6 tablespoons olive oil · 1 teaspoon salt ·**

Cook the parsley in a cup of water until tender. Drain and set aside. Put the almonds, vinegar, olive oil, and salt in a blender. Blend at medium speed for 2 or 3 minutes. Combine the blended mixture with the parsley and serve as a topping for any baked or broiled fish.

MAKES ABOUT 2 CUPS.

antojitos

7

tortillas, burritos, enchiladas, tamales, chalupas, beans, chili, chiles, and tacos

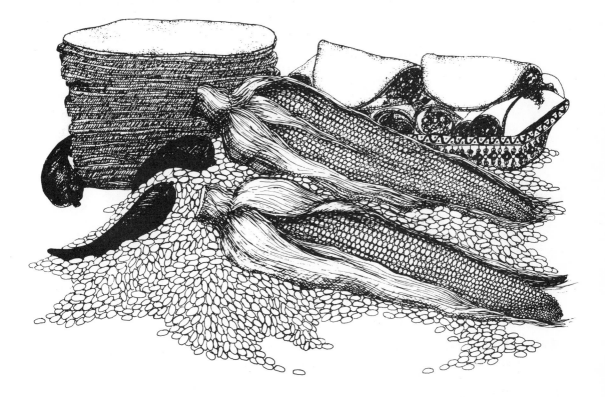

When we think of Mexican food, we cannot help but mentally picture tacos, enchiladas, tamales, tostadas, beans, and chiles. The Mexicans use a term grouping all of these under one word— "antojitos." Look up the noun "antojo" in a Spanish dictionary, and you will find: "whim," "notion," "fancy." "Antojitos" is the diminutive plural and is a Mexican term not used in other Spanish-speaking countries in the way it is meant in Mexico. No one really knows how the term originated, but it goes back hundreds of years. It means a snack, and it is usually served in the late afternoon or evening. All over Mexico, many small but very famous restaurants specialize in antojitos. The recipes in this chapter may be served as antojitos for a snack or as the main course. We will start with tortillas, for they really are typical of Mexico and are usually served at every meal. Although in the past all tortillas were made of corn, tortillas made of flour are very popular now. Both corn and flour tortillas can be purchased in supermarkets in the United States today, or you can make them yourself.

Tortilla de Maiz

Corn Tortillas

Corn tortillas are made from dehydrated masa flour called "Masa Harina," which, in the United States, is made by the Quaker Oats Company.

2 cups dehydrated masa flour ·
1 teaspoon salt ·
1/4 cup shortening ·
1 cup warm water (approximately) ·

Put flour in mixing bowl; sprinkle with salt and stir to mix; cut in the shortening until the particles are fine. Add warm water gradually (one cup may be too much) until the dough is firm and will not stick to your fingers.

The dough may be refrigerated before using for as long as 24 hours by greasing the surface and covering tightly with foil or plastic wrap. The dough is easier to handle if it has been refrigerated.

Divide the dough into 12 equal-sized pieces. Shape into small balls about 1-1/4 inches in diameter. If you are using a tortilla press, pat the balls (one at a time) in the press between two pieces of waxed paper. Press slowly and firmly on lever until the tortilla measures 6 inches in diameter. If you do not have a press, put each ball of dough between two pieces of waxed paper and roll with a rolling pin until the tortilla measures 6 inches in diameter. You may have to trim the tortilla to a round shape.

Carefully remove the top piece of waxed paper. Drop the tortilla, wax paper side up, onto a hot, ungreased griddle. Carefully remove the other piece of wax paper. Cook the tortillas about one minute on each side until they are a delicate brown. Be careful not to burn them.

Tortillas are delicious served warm with butter as a substitute for bread or rolls; and they are a necessary ingredient for making all types of enchiladas, chalupas, burritos, tacos, and tostados.

MAKES 12 TORTILLAS.

Tortillas de Harina

Flour Tortillas

2 cups unsifted white flour · 1 teaspon salt · 1/4 cup shortening · 1/2 cup warm water ·

Put flour in mixing bowl; sprinkle with salt; stir to mix. With pastry blender or two knives, cut in shortening until particles are fine. Add water gradually; toss on a lightly floured board with a fork to make a stiff dough. Form into a ball and knead thoroughly until the dough is smooth and flecked with air bubbles.

You may grease the surface of the dough, cover tightly, and refrigerate for as long as 24 hours before using; the dough is easier to handle if you do this. Allow the dough to return to room temperature before you begin to roll it out.

Divide the dough into 12 balls and roll with a rolling pin between sheets of waxed paper until they are 7 or 8 inches in diameter. Although corn tortillas are about 6 inches in diameter, floured tortillas are 7 inches or more across. In some areas of Mexico, floured tortillas will be as large as 18 inches in diameter.

If you are using a tortilla press, proceed as you would for corn tortillas, by putting the balls of dough (one at a time) in the press between two pieces of waxed paper. Press slowly and firmly on lever until the tortilla measures 7 inches or more in diameter.

Carefully remove the top piece of waxed paper. Drop the tortilla wax paper side up onto a hot, ungreased griddle. Carefully remove the other piece of wax paper. Cook about 20 seconds on one side. Flip over with a spatula and bake on the other side. Serve at once with butter, or try any of the following recipes calling for flour tortillas.

MAKES 12 TORTILLAS.

Burritos con Hamburguesa

Burritos (Little Donkeys) with Hamburger

1 pound ground
beef ·
1/2 medium-sized
onion, chopped ·
2 tablespoons
vegetable or olive
oil · 1 tablespoon
chili powder ·
1 teaspoon salt ·
1/2 teaspoon garlic
salt · 1/4 teaspoon
tabasco sauce ·
2 medium-sized
tomatoes, peeled
and chopped or
1-16 ounce can
tomatoes drained
and chopped ·
10-12 flour
tortillas ·

Brown ground beef with onion in the oil until the onion is soft. Drain fat. Add all ingredients except tortillas and simmer 30 minutes.

Warm the flour tortillas in a 325° oven for 10 minutes.

MAKES 10 OR 12 BURRITOS.

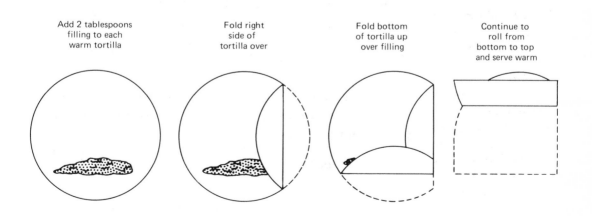

Add 2 tablespoons filling to each warm tortilla

Fold right side of tortilla over

Fold bottom of tortilla up over filling

Continue to roll from bottom to top and serve warm

Burritos con Frijoles, Queso y Chilies

Burritos with Beans, Cheese, and Chili Filling

2 cups refried beans · 1/2 medium-sized onion, chopped · 1 teaspoon chili powder · 1/2 teaspoon salt · 1/2 teaspoon garlic salt · 1/4 teaspoon tabasco sauce · 1-4 ounce can green chiles, chopped · 4 ounces monterey jack cheese, shredded · 10 flour tortillas ·

Simmer refried beans with onion for 10 minutes. Add remaining ingredients, except tortillas, and heat thoroughly.

Warm the flour tortillas in a 325° oven for 10 minutes.

Add 2 large tablespoons of the filling to each flour tortilla. Follow instructions in "Burritos with Hamburger" recipe for folding tortillas.

MAKES 10 BURRITOS.

Burritos con Chorizo y Frijoles

Burritos with Sausage and Beans

1 pound chorizo or ground sausage, seasoned hot · 1 medium-sized onion, chopped · 2 cups refried beans · 2 tablespoons taco sauce · 1/2 teaspoon garlic salt · 1/4 teaspoon salt · 1/2 cup cheddar cheese, grated · 10 flour tortillas ·

If you are using chorizo sausage, remove the casings. Fry the sausage with the onion until the onion is soft. Drain. Add all of the remaining ingredients except the tortillas and simmer 20 minutes.

Warm the flour tortillas in a 325° oven for 10 minutes.

Add 2 tablespoons of filling to each warm tortilla. Follow instructions in "Burritos with Hamburger" recipe for folding tortillas.

MAKES 10 BURRITOS.

In Mexico, enchiladas are served as soon as the ingredients are put together. In the United States, it is more common for the sake of convenience to pour more sauce over the enchiladas and keep them hot in a warming oven. In this way, the enchiladas can be made in advance and reheated at the last minute.

In all of the following enchilada recipes, be careful not to fry the tortillas crisp. In addition, if you do put the dish in the oven before serving, take care not to dry out the tortillas.

Enchiladas de Frijoles

Bean Enchiladas

12 corn tortillas · 1-1/2 cups refried beans · 1/4 cup vegetable oil · 1 cup sour cream ·

Spread the tortillas with the refried beans. Roll and hold them together with toothpicks. Fry in oil until they are a golden brown. Place the tortillas in an ungreased shallow baking dish. Bake at 325° for fifteen minutes. Two minutes before removing from the oven, top with the sour cream.

MAKES 12 ENCHILADAS.

Enchiladas Rojas

Red Enchiladas

6 ancho chiles or 1 cup bell or green peppers, chopped · 3 medium-sized tomatoes (peeled, seeded, and chopped) · 2 medium-sized onions, chopped · 2 cloves garlic, chopped · 6 tablespoons vegetable oil · 1/2 teaspoon salt · 1/4 teaspoon pepper · 1/2 teaspoon sugar · 1 cup light cream · 2 beaten eggs · 6 chorizo sausages, skinned and chopped, or 1 pound ground sausage, seasoned hot · 1/2 cup sharp cheddar cheese, grated · 24 corn tortillas ·

Wash the chiles, if you are using them, and remove veins, stems, and seeds. Chop them and soak them in a cup of hot water for an hour.

In the blender, combine the tomatoes, one of the chopped onions, garlic, and the chiles with a little of their water and blend, making a smooth purée. Heat 2 tablespoons of the oil in a skillet; add the purée and cook over medium heat, stirring continually for five minutes. Season to taste with sugar, salt, and pepper. Stir in the beaten eggs and cream. Remove from the fire and set aside.

Sauté the sausages in a little more oil until they are brown. Drain. Add a third of the sauce mixture and a third of the grated cheese to the sausages.

Dip the tortillas one by one in the sauce and fry on both sides in about 3 tablespoons of hot oil until they are limp. Place a little of the sausage mixture on each tortilla. Roll the tortilla and place (flap side down) in an ungreased baking dish. Place the filled enchiladas side by side in the dish. Pour the remaining sauce over them and sprinkle the remaining cheese on top. Bake, uncovered, at 325° for about thirty minutes.

MAKES 24 ENCHILADAS.

Enchiladas de Chile Colorado

Enchiladas with Red Chile

10 large red chiles ·
1 cup milk · 2 eggs,
well-beaten ·
1/2 teaspoon salt ·
1/4 teaspoon black
pepper · 1 pound
ground sausage ·
1 cup cooked
potatoes, chopped ·
1 cup tomatoes,
peeled and chopped
or 1 cup canned
tomatoes ·
2 medium-sized
onions, chopped ·
3/4 cup sharp
cheddar cheese,
grated · 1/4 cup
vegetable oil ·
24 tortillas ·

Devein and remove the seeds from the chiles. Soak the chiles in warm water for an hour unless you are using canned chiles. Chop the chiles; mix them with a cup of milk, two beaten eggs, and 1/4 teaspoon salt.

Brown the sausage in a frying pan. Drain and set aside. In the same pan, fry the potatoes, tomatoes, one of the onions, 1/4 teaspoon salt, and 1/4 teaspoon pepper. When the onion begins to brown, return the sausage to the pan and cook until the mixture is dry. Add 1/4 cup of grated cheese.

Fry each tortilla (one at a time) in the oil for a few seconds until it is limp, but not crisp. Soak each tortilla in the milk mixture.

Spoon about 3 tablespoons of the sausage mixture down the center of the tortilla. Sprinkle with a little of the remaining chopped onion and grated cheese. Roll the tortilla and place (flap side down) in an ungreased baking dish. Use toothpicks to hold tortillas together if necessary. Place the filled enchiladas side by side in the dish. Pour the remaining sauce and milk mixture with the chiles over the top of the enchiladas. Top with the remainder of the cheese. Bake, uncovered, at 325° for twenty minutes.

MAKES 24 ENCHILADAS.

Enchiladas Verdes

Green Enchiladas

2-1/2 cups commercial green sauce · 12 corn tortillas · 2 tablespoons vegetable oil · 2 medium-sized onions · 1/2 cup sharp cheddar cheese, shredded · 1 cup sour cream ·

Heat the green sauce. In a skillet, fry the tortillas (one at a time) in the oil for a few seconds until they are limp, but not crisp. Drain.

Dip each tortilla in green sauce. Place flat tortilla in ungreased shallow baking dish. Top each tortilla with chopped onion, cheese, and a teaspoon of sour cream. Stack the next layer of tortillas on top of the first, and continue the layers until all the tortillas are in the baking dish. Pour any remaining sauce, onions, cheese, and sour cream over the stacks. Heat at 325° for 20 minutes.

MAKES 12 ENCHILADAS.

Enchiladas de Pechuga de Pollo

Chicken Breast Enchiladas

2 cups cooked and boned chicken (2 large chicken breasts) · 6 green chiles, chopped · 1 tablespoon almonds, blanched and chopped · 1 tablespoon chopped green olives · 12 tortillas · 2 eggs, beaten · 1/2 cup vegetable oil · 4 large tomatoes, peeled and chopped · 1/2 onion, chopped · 1/2 teaspoon salt · 1/4 teaspoon pepper · 1-1/2 onions sliced · lettuce leaves · 1 bunch of radishes ·

Boil chicken breasts in water; cover, and cook until tender. Bone and dice. Mix chicken, chiles, almonds, and olives together. Dip the tortillas (one at a time) in the eggs. Put about 2 tablespoons of the chicken mixture on each one, roll and hold them together with toothpicks. Fry in hot oil for a few seconds. Place the filled enchiladas side by side in an ungreased baking dish.

In the oil that remains, fry the tomatoes, the chopped half of the onion, salt, and pepper until the onion is soft but not brown. Pour this mixture over the enchiladas. Bake uncovered in a 325° oven for 30 minutes. Serve hot, garnishing the platter with onion slices, whole lettuce leaves, and radishes, cut into "flowers."

MAKES 12 ENCHILADAS.

Enchiladas Rellenas de Sardina

Enchiladas Stuffed with Sardines

24 corn tortillas (frozen tortillas may be substituted) · **1/4 cup vegetable or olive oil, or lard** · **2 medium-sized onions, chopped** · **1 potato, cooked and chopped** · **3 large tomatoes, peeled and chopped** · **1 garlic clove, chopped** · **8 ancho chiles (or substitute 1 4-ounce can green chiles)** · **1 teaspoon salt** · **1/4 teaspoon pepper** · **1 3-3/4 ounce can sardines with oil** · **1 cup light cream** · **3/4 cup sharp cheddar cheese, grated** ·

Fry the tortillas in the oil or lard (Mexicans would use lard) over medium heat for a few seconds until the tortillas are limp but not crisp. Drain on paper towels.

In the same oil, fry onions, potato, tomatoes, garlic, chiles, salt, and pepper until the onion is soft. Chop the sardines and add to the mixture.

Dip each tortilla in cream and fill with two heaping tablespoons of the sardine mixture. Roll the tortilla and hold it together with toothpicks if necessary. Place tortillas side by side in a shallow glass baking dish. Top with any remaining cream and the cheese. Bake at 350° for twenty minutes or until hot throughout.

MAKES 24 ENCHILADAS.

Enchiladas de Res Enrolladas

Rolled Meat Enchiladas

1 pound ground beef · 1 medium-sized onion, chopped · 1/2 cup red chili sauce or canned enchilada sauce · 16 corn tortillas · 1/4 cup vegetable oil · 3/4 cup onion, chopped · 3 cups sharp cheddar cheese, grated ·

Brown the ground beef in a frying pan with the medium-sized chopped onion until the onion is soft. Drain. Add 1/2 cup of the chili sauce or enchilada sauce and simmer for 10 minutes, stirring occasionally. Set aside.

Fry each tortilla in a little oil for a few seconds until it begins to blister and is limp, but not crisp. Remove and dip into heated red sauce; then place in baking dish.

Spoon about 3 tablespoons of the ground beef mixture down the center of the tortilla; sprinkle with about 2 teaspoons of chopped onion and 2 tablespoons of cheese. Roll the tortilla and place (flap side down) in the ungreased baking dish. Place the filled enchiladas side by side in the pan. Pour the remaining sauce over them and sprinkle the remaining cheese on top. Bake, uncovered, at 325° for twenty minutes.

MAKES 16 ENCHILADAS.

Tamales are not anything new in the United States. Many towns had their "Hot Tamale Pete" or "Hot Tamale Joe" who sold his wares from push carts not much unlike those seen in Mexico. The main difference is that tamales in this country are more or less uniform in size and contain a meat filling. Mexican tamales differ in size and include a wide variety of fillings of meats, fruits, or sweets.

Masa para Tamales

Masa Dough for Tamales

24 dried cornhusks, or substitute ·
24 sheets of foil ·
1/2 cup lard ·
3 cups dehydrated masa flour or white corn meal ·
1/2 teaspoon baking powder ·
1/2 teaspoon salt ·
1-1/4 cups warm water, meat, or chicken stock ·

Fresh cornhusks are used in Mexico. These are available wherever you live, for the produce manager of the supermarket probably will be glad to save some for you. If you do need to substitute, use baking paper or foil cut in 5 by 10 inch pieces or much smaller if you are preparing "antojitos." If you do use cornhusks, cover them with hot water and let them soak for 30 minutes. Drain and pat dry.

Try to find the dehydrated masa flour. Refer to the recipe for corn tortillas on page 74. This masa flour is sold in many areas of the United States. If you are unable to find it, substitute white corn meal, although the tamales will not be the same.

To make the dough, whip the lard (do not use a substitute) until bubbles form. Blend in the masa flour (or corn meal), baking powder, and salt; slowly add the warm water or broth. Continue to beat for 4 or 5 more minutes. If you wish to test the dough, drop a small piece in water. If it floats, the dough is ready to assemble.

Place about a tablespoon of dough in the center of the cornhusk, paper, or foil. Spread the dough out until it reaches almost to the edge of the husk or paper. Put a large tablespoon of filling in the center of the dough. Any of the following tamale recipes may be used for the filling. Fold the right side of the husk slightly over half the filling; fold the left side until the dough meets. Fold the top and bottom up toward the center. Stack the tamales on a rack or colander in a deep pan to which water has been added. Be sure the tamales do not touch the water, but bring the water to a boil, cover the pan, lower the heat, and steam the tamales for one hour. Remove with tongs and serve hot.

Tamales may be assembled and frozen for a month or more before steaming. They also may be assembled, steamed, and refrigerated for a week. Reheat for about 30 minutes before serving.

MAKES 24 TAMALES.

Tamales de Pollo

Chicken Tamales

2 four-pound baking hens · 1 teaspoon salt · 2 ancho chiles, dried · 2 mulato chiles, dried · 2 pasillo chiles, dried (or substitute 1 large bell pepper and 2 small hot peppers) · 2 cups chicken stock · 1/2 cup almonds, blanched · 1 medium-sized onion, chopped · 3 medium-sized tomatoes, peeled and chopped, or 1 cup canned tomatoes, drained · 2 tablespoons sesame seeds · 1 garlic clove, chopped · 1/2 teaspoon ground cinnamon · 1/2 teaspoon ground cloves · 1/2 teaspoon ground coriander · 1 teaspoon salt · 1/4 teaspoon black pepper · 1 cup chicken broth · 24 cornhusks ·

The dough and corn husks should be prepared according to directions for "Masa Dough for Tamales" on page 86.

Put the chickens in a large pot. Add the salt and enough water to cover the chickens. Bring to a boil. Reduce heat to simmer; cover the pan; cook for one hour.

Prepare the filling by removing the stems and seeds from the chiles or bell pepper. Chop and put in a bowl. Pour two cups of chicken stock over them and soak twenty minutes.

Blend the almonds in an electric blender until they are pulverized. Add the chiles and the chicken stock to the blender. Blend slowly for one minute. Then add to the blender the onion, tomatoes, sesame seeds, garlic, cinnamon, cloves, coriander, salt, and pepper. Blend at high speed until the mixture has the consistency of a purée.

Remove the bones and skin from the chickens and chop the meat. Reserve the broth. Combine the chicken and the blended mixture in a skillet and simmer with about one cup of the chicken broth for about thirty minutes or until the liquid is consumed.

Drop about two tablespoons of the filling in the center of the dough. Fold the right side of the husk slightly over half the filling; fold the left side until the dough meets. Fold the top and bottom up toward the center. Steam the tamales for one hour following the directions for "Masa Dough for Tamales."

MAKES 24 LARGE OR ABOUT 50 SMALL TAMALES.

Tamales de Carne de Puerco

Pork Meat Tamales

Follow the preceding recipe for "Chicken Tamales," but substitute two cups of cooked pork loin which has been diced. If you have both cooked chicken and cooked pork on hand, use one cup of each. It is not unusual to use both pork and chicken in the same dish in Mexico.

Tamales de Hamburguesa

Ground Beef Tamales

1 pound ground beef · 1/2 medium-sized onion, diced · 2 tablespoons vegetable or olive oil · 1 tablespoon chili powder · 1 teaspoon salt · 1/2 teaspoon garlic salt · 1/4 teaspoon tabasco sauce · 2 medium-sized tomatoes, peeled and chopped or 1-16 ounce can tomatoes, drained and chopped ·

Prepare dough and corn husks according to directions for "Masa Dough for Tamales" on page 86.

Brown the ground beef with the onion in oil until the onion is soft. Drain fat. Add all of the ingredients and simmer for 30 minutes or until the mixture is dry.

Drop a heaping tablespoon of the filling in the center of the dough. Fold the right side of the husk slightly over half the filing; fold the left side until the dough meets. Fold the top and bottom up toward the center. Steam the tamales for one hour following directions for "Masa Dough for Tamales."

MAKES 24 TAMALES.

Tamales de Almendra

Almond Tamales

1 cup (8 ounces) butter · 1-1/4 cups white granulated sugar · 1 cup almonds, blanched · 1 cup milk · 4 cups dehydrated masa flour or white corn meal · 1/2 cup rice flour; or, if unavailable, add an additional 1/2 cup masa or corn meal · 1 teaspoon baking powder · 24 dried cornhusks, or substitute sheets of foil ·

Soak the cornhusks in hot water for 30 minutes. Dry them with paper towels.

Whip the butter until it is nearly white. If you are using an electric mixer, beat about ten minutes at medium speed, or twenty minutes by hand. Mix the sugar and almonds with the milk and add to the butter.

Sift the flour with the baking powder and blend with the butter mixture. Continue to beat for 4 or 5 more minutes.

On each cornhusk or foil, place about a tablespoon of dough and spread until it reaches almost to the edge of the husk or paper.

Filling:

5 egg yolks, beaten · 1 cup sugar · 1/2 teaspoon cinnamon · 2 tablespoons flour · 2 cups milk ·

Beat all the ingredients together. Cook over a low fire, stirring continually for about 30 minutes, or until the mixture is thick. Allow to cool before stuffing the tamales.

Then add a heaping tablespoon of filling to the dough. Follow the instructions in the recipe "Masa Dough for Tamales" on page 86 by folding the right side of husk; then by folding the left side and the ends. Steam the tamales for an hour.

MAKES 24 TAMALES.

Tamales de Coco

Coconut Tamales

Follow the preceding recipe for "Almond Tamales," omitting the almonds from the dough.

Filling:

1 cup shredded coconut · 1/4 cup raisins · 1 cup preserves or jam (strawberry, apricot, or pineapple) ·

Mix the filling ingredients. Stuff the tamales according to the "Almond Tamales" recipe, and steam cook for one hour.

MAKES 24 TAMALES.

Tamales de Elote

Corn Tamales

Follow the recipe for "Masa Dough for Tamales" on page 86.

Filling:

1 tablespoon butter · 2 jalapeño chiles · 1/2 teaspoon salt · 1/4 teaspoon pepper · 2 cups canned tomatoes · 1 medium-sized onion, chopped · 12 ounce can whole kernel corn, drained ·

In the butter, fry the deveined chiles, which have been cut in thin strips, with the salt, pepper, tomatoes and chopped onion. Simmer until the onion is tender. Add the corn; continue to simmer until the mixture is thick.

Follow the recipe for "Masa Dough for Tamales" by placing a large tablespoon of filling in the center of the dough, and steaming the tamales for one hour.

MAKES 24 TAMALES.

If you look up the word "chalupa" in a Spanish-to-English dictionary, you will find the meaning "a small lifeboat" or the Spanish-American meaning of "corncake." Mexicans added their own flare to the term named after the boats in the floating gardens of Xochimilco, a tourist attraction near Mexico City. In Mexico, a chalupa is the dough of a tortilla, shaped like little boats and filled with various fillings.

Chalupas del D. F.

Mexico City Chalupas

Prepare the dough from dehydrated masa flour according to the recipe at the beginning of this chapter on page 74. Divide the dough into 16 equal parts.

Pat each part of the dehydrated masa dough into an oval shape about four inches long.

Fry the ovals on a medium-hot ungreased griddle or frying pan until the dough starts to harden. Drain on paper towels, and lift the side of the dough in the shape of a small boat.

1 cup ground beef ·
1 cup green
tomatoes,
chopped · 2 green
mountain chiles, or
2 jalapeño
peppers · 1 clove
garlic, diced ·
1/4 medium-sized
onion, chopped ·
1/4 teaspoon salt ·

Prepare a sauce with the ground beef, tomatoes, chiles, garlic, onion, and salt. Simmer for thirty minutes. Place some of the sauce in each chalupa boat. Garnish with shredded lettuce if you desire.

MAKES 16 CHALUPAS.

Chalupas de Estado de Morelos

Chalupas from the State of Morelos

Prepare the dough from dehydrated masa flour according to the recipe at the beginning of this chapter on page 74. Divide the dough into 16 equal parts. Pat each part of the masa dough into an oval shape about four inches long.

Fry the ovals on a medium-hot ungreased griddle or frying pan until dough begins to harden. Drain on paper towels, and lift the sides of the dough in the shape of small boat.

1-1/2 cups cooked pork, diced · 1/2 cup onion, chopped · 2 tablespoons vegetable oil · 1 cup sharp Cheddar cheese, grated · hot sauce ·

Simmer the onion and the pork in oil until the onion is soft. Drain. Add this mixture to each small "boat"; top with the cheese, and serve with your favorite hot sauce as a side dish.

MAKES 16 CHALUPAS.

Chalupas Poblanas

Puebla-Style Chalupas

Prepare the dough from dehydrated masa flour according to the recipe at the beginning of this chapter on page 74. Divide the dough into 24 equal parts. Pat each part of the masa dough into an oval shape. Fry on medium-hot ungreased griddle or in frying pan until dough begins to harden. Drain on paper towels, and lift the sides of the dough to form a small boat.

1/4 cup vegetable or olive oil · 1 medium-sized onion, chopped · 2 cloves garlic, chopped · 3 mountain chiles, or 3 small hot green chiles, chopped · 1 cup green tomatoes, chopped · 1/4 teaspoon salt · 1 cup cooked pork, diced · 1/2 cup sharp Cheddar cheese, grated ·

Fry the onion and garlic in the oil until the onion is soft. Add the chiles, tomatoes, and salt. Simmer for thirty minutes. Add the cooked pork; simmer until the pork is hot. Spoon some of the mixture into each of the 24 "boats." Top with grated cheese, and serve with your favorite hot sauce as a side dish.

MAKES 24 SMALL CHALUPAS.

In Mexico, the diets of the upper and lower classes are quite different. The moneyed class can afford to buy protein-rich foods, but the lower classes consume low-cost beans and tortillas almost exclusively. The following bean recipes are a "must" among the higher classes as the last course of the "comida."

Frijoles Refritos

Refried Beans

1 pound dried pinto
beans · 6 cups
water ·
1 medium-sized
onion, diced ·
1/2 cup butter, or
bacon drippings ·
1 teaspoon salt ·

Soak the beans in cold water overnight. Drain, and cook them, with the sliced onion, in enough fresh water to cover—about six cups. Simmer until the beans are soft, about three hours. Add butter or bacon drippings and salt. While the beans continue to cook on low heat, mash them with a potato masher (or as the Mexican women do, with a wooden spoon). Continue to cook until the mixture is thick enough to be rolled into a ball. Add more salt if necessary. Serve immediately; or the mixture can be refrigerated for several weeks and reheated.

MAKES 6 CUPS.

Serving suggestions:

Refried beans are typical of Mexico and can be used as a filling for enchiladas, burritos, chalupas, chiles, tacos, or as a side vegetable dish.

They are delicious as a dip served with tortillas or corn chips. For variety, mix one cup of refried beans with three chopped Jalapeño peppers, or if you like a milder dip, mix one cup of refried beans with one cup of sour cream. Serve warm.

Frijoles Estilo Mejicano

Mexican-Style Beans

1 pound dried pinto beans · 6 cups water · 1 medium-sized onion, diced · 1/4 cup butter, or bacon drippings · 1 teaspoon salt, or salt to taste ·

Soak the beans in cold water overnight. Drain, and cook them, covered, with the sliced onion, in about six cups of fresh cold water. Simmer slowly for about two hours. Add the butter or bacon drippings, and salt. Simmer for about one more hour, but remove from the heat when they are soft. More salt may have to be added, and the bean broth should be thick. Serve hot.

MAKES 8–10 SERVINGS.

Enfrijoladas Veracruzanas

Veracruz Bean Tortillas

1 medium-sized onion, chopped · 2 tablespoons butter or vegetable oil · 1 pound ground pork sausage · 3 cups refried beans · 1 teaspoon salt · 1/4 cup vegetable oil · 12 corn tortillas ·

Sauté the onion in two tablespoons of butter or oil in a frying pan until soft. Add the sausage; fry it thoroughly. Remove the sausage and onion from the pan. Reserve about two tablespoons of grease in the pan, and simmer the refried beans and salt until the mixture is hot. Stir occasionally.

Fry the tortillas in a separate frying pan in vegetable oil until they begin to brown. Drain on paper towels. Spread each tortilla with the bean and sausage mixture and serve warm.

MAKES 12 TORTILLAS.

Chile con Carne

Chile with Meat

2 pounds ground beef · 2 cups water · 1 tablespoon salt · 5 ancho chiles, or substitute three bell peppers, chopped · 1 tablespoon chili powder (optional) · 2 garlic cloves, chopped · 1 large onion, chopped · 1 15-ounce can pinto or chili beans ·

Simmer the meat in two cups of water with the salt for 40 minutes. Devein the chiles; soak them in hot water for 30 minutes. Chop the chiles, (if you use a bell pepper, add chili powder); and add the chiles, garlic, onion, and oregano to the meat; simmer until the mixture is thick. Add the canned beans and serve hot.

MAKES 6 CUPS.

Chile con Carne de Puerco

Chile with Pork Meat

2 pounds lean cooked pork, cut in 1 inch cubes · 1 tablespoon vegetable cooking oil · 2 tablespoons flour · 1 tablespoon chili powder · 2 cups water · 1 teaspoon sugar · 1/2 teaspoon ground cumin (comino) · 1 garlic clove, chopped · 4 cups tomatoes or enchilada sauce · 1 tablespoon salt · 1/2 teaspoon pepper · 1 15-ounce can pinto or chili beans

Brown the pork in the oil. Stir in the flour and chili powder. Slowly add the water, stirring continually, with pan on low heat. Add sugar, cumin, garlic, tomatoes or sauce, salt, and pepper. Bring to a boil; then lower the fire to simmer. Cover and simmer for two hours. Just before serving, add the beans.

MAKES 6 CUPS.

Chiles Rellenos

Stuffed Chiles

8 whole green chile peppers, or 2 4-ounce cans of whole green chiles · 1 cup sharp cheddar cheese, cut in strips · 2 onions, chopped · 1 cup lard or shortening · 2 cups cooked pork, chopped · 12 large green olives, chopped · 1/2 teaspoon salt · 1/4 teaspoon pepper · 1/2 cup water · 4 eggs, separated · flour for coating ·

Cut peppers lengthwise and remove seeds. Stuff each chile with cheese strips. Brown onion in two tablespoons of lard; add cooked pork, olives, salt, pepper and water; simmer for thirty minutes.

Stuff each chile with some of the pork mixture. Beat the egg whites and yolks separately; then fold together. Coat each pepper with flour; then dip into egg mixture and deep fat fry in the rest of the shortening until golden brown on both sides. Drain on paper towels. Serve immediately. These may be served with your favorite hot sauce as a side dish.

MAKES 8 STUFFED CHILES.

Chiles Relleno de Queso

Chiles Stuffed with Cheese

8 whole green chile peppers, or 2 4-ounce cans whole green chiles · 1 cup Romano cheese, cut in strips · 3/4 cup refried beans · 4 eggs, separated · 1 tablespoon water · 1/2 teaspoon salt · 1/4 teaspoon pepper · 4 tablespoons flour · 1/2 cup lard or shortening ·

Cut a slit in each chile. Insert a tablespoon of beans and strips of cheese (the more the better), and close the slit.

Separate the egg whites and yolks. Beat the egg whites to a peak. Beat the egg yolks well with water, salt, and pepper. Fold the egg yolks with the egg whites; then fold flour into the egg mixture.

Dip each chile in the batter, and fry in the hot lard or shortening, which should be about 1/2 inch deep in the frying pan. Turn the chiles until both sides are a golden brown. Do not crowd them in the pan. Drain on a paper towel. Serve hot, either plain or with your favorite sauce.

MAKES 8 STUFFED CHILES.

Chile Relleno Lujo

Stuffed Chiles Supreme

8 whole green chile peppers, or 2 4-ounce cans whole green chiles · 1/2 pound sharp cheddar cheese, diced · 4 eggs, separated · flour for coating · 1/2 cup lard or shortening ·

Cut a slit in each chile. Stuff with cheese. Separate the egg whites and yolks. Beat the egg whites to a peak. Beat the egg yolks; fold into the egg whites. Dip each chile in flour, then in the egg mixture, and fry in hot lard on both sides until a golden brown. Drain on paper towels and set aside.

1/2 medium onion, chopped · 1 garlic clove, minced · 1 tablespoon vegetable or olive oil · 1 cup chicken broth · 1-1/2 cups canned tomatoes, drained and chopped · 1 tablespoon chili powder · 1/2 teaspoon oregano · 1/4 teaspoon ground cumin (comino) · 1/2 teaspoon salt · 1/4 teaspoon black pepper · 1/4 cup sharp cheddar cheese, diced ·

For the supreme sauce:

Sauté onion and garlic in hot oil; add broth, tomatoes, chili powder, oregano, cumin, salt, and pepper. Simmer ten minutes.

Preheat oven to 350°. Place the chiles flat in an oven-proof pan. Top with the supreme sauce and the cheese. Heat until the cheese is melted, and serve immediately.

MAKES 8 CHILES.

There are two types of tacos served in Mexico; one is soft and one is fried crisp. For a soft taco, which is very popular among the Indians, gently fry a tortilla on one side and then on the other, just as the enchiladas are fried, but in a lightly oiled frying pan. Fold in the shape of a half circle and stuff with your favorite filling. For a crispy taco, fry in deep fat, placing a knife or spatula down the center of the tortilla while it is frying to make it turn up in the shape of a semi-circle. It is also possible to use a taco press for frying crispy tacos, or to buy them in your grocery store already fried. When the tortilla is crisp, remove from the fire and drain on paper towels. Fill with any of the following stuffings.

Tacos de Frijoles

Bean Tacos

12 tortillas ·
1/2 cup lard or
shortening · 2 cups
refried beans ·
shortening ·
shredded lettuce ·
1/2 cup sharp
cheddar cheese,
shredded · 1/2 cup
onions, chopped ·
sauce (optional) ·

Prepare the tortillas according to the preceding recipe for tacos. Drain on paper towels. If the taco shells are already prepared, place in a 225° oven and heat for five minutes.

Heat the refried beans and spoon this filling into each of the tortillas. Top with shredded lettuce, cheese, and chopped onions. Serve with sauce as a side dish if you desire.

MAKES 12 TACOS.

Tacos de Hamburguesa

Beef Tacos

12 tortillas ·
1/2 cup lard or
shortening ·
1 pound hamburger
1/2 medium-sized
onion · 3 large
tomatoes, peeled
and chopped ·
lettuce, shredded ·
Cheddar cheese,
shredded · sauce
(optional) ·

Prepare the tortillas according to the recipe for tacos on page 102. Drain on paper towels. If the taco shells are already prepared, place in a 225° oven and heat for five minutes.

Simmer hamburger, onion, and tomatoes for 20 minutes. Spoon filling in each taco shell, and top with shredded lettuce and cheese. Serve with your favorite sauce as a side dish if you desire.

MAKES 12 TACOS.

Tacos con Pollo

Chicken Tacos

12 tortillas ·
1/2 cup onion,
chopped ·
2 tablespoons lard
or butter · 2 cups
cooked chicken,
diced ·
1/2 teaspoon salt ·
1/4 teaspoon
pepper ·
1/4 teaspoon garlic
salt · lettuce,
shredded · 1/4 cup
Cheddar cheese,
shredded ·
24 whole radishes ·

Prepare the tortillas according to the recipe for tacos on page 102. Drain on paper towels. If the taco shells are already prepared, place in a 225° oven and heat for five minutes.

Sauté the onion in the lard or butter until the onion is soft. Add chicken, salt, pepper, and garlic salt. Simmer for fifteen minutes.

Fill tacos with the chicken mixture. Serve side dishes of lettuce, cheese, whole radishes, and your favorite sauce if you desire.

MAKES 12 TACOS.

el pescado

8

sea food

At the time the Spaniards arrived in Mexico at Montezuma's court, fish was an important part of the gourmet diet. Because they came from Spain, a country nearly surrounded by water, sea food was nothing new to the Spaniards, but the Mexicans' art of preparation was new. Today, each region has its sea food specialty, and often the recipes are a well-guarded secret.

Escabeche de Pescado

Pickled Fish

2-1/2 pounds fish steaks (cod, perch, halibut, or flounder) · 5 lemons · 1 medium-sized tomato, peeled and chopped · 1 medium-sized onion, chopped · 3 mountain chiles, or any variety of red or green hot peppers · 1/2 teaspoon ground coriander · 1/2 teaspoon salt · 20 black olives · 1 avocado, peeled and sliced · saltine crackers ·

Cut the fish into bite size pieces and marinate in the juice of five lemons overnight in the refrigerator. Add tomato, onion, chiles, coriander, and salt; marinate two more hours. Pickled fish improves with more marinating. If you want to refrigerate this dish for a week before serving, it will increase in flavor. Serve cold in cocktail cups, garnished with olives, avocado, a slice of lemon, and crackers.

SERVES 10.

Escabeche Veracruzano

Veracruz-Style Pickled Fish

2-1/2 pounds fish filets (perch, halibut, or flounder) · 1/2 cup olive oil or vegetable oil · 1 large onion, chopped · 1/2 cup vinegar · 1 teaspoon salt · 1/4 teaspoon black pepper · 1/2 teaspoon ground coriander · 1/4 teaspoon cinnamon · 1 bay leaf · 2 lemons, sliced ·

Clean the filets; slice in serving pieces. Fry in oil over a low fire until they are brown. Place filets in shallow glass casserole dish. In a frying pan, sauté the onion until it is soft. Mix the onion with vinegar, salt, pepper, coriander, cinnamon, and bay leaf. Pour this mixture over the filets. Top the fish with the lemon slices.

Marinate in the refrigerator for four or five days before serving. Serve cold.

SERVES 8–10.

Pescado en Adobo Especial

Special Pickled Fish

2 pounds fish filets (perch, halibut, or flounder) · 1/2 cup olive or vegetable oil · 1 cup vinegar · 2 lemons · 1 bay leaf · 1/2 teaspoon dried thyme · 1/2 teaspoon leaf oregano · 1/2 teaspoon salt · 3 garlic cloves ·

Fry the fish filets in the oil over medium heat for five minutes. Place filets in shallow casserole dish. Mix the spices with the garlic, vinegar, and juice of two lemons. Pour vinegar mixture over fish and refrigerate for several hours. Serve cold.

SERVES 8.

Cebiche Estilo Acapulco

Acapulco-Style Pickled Fish

2 pounds salpa (or
substitute perch,
halibut, or flounder
filets) · 5 lemons ·
2 medium-sized
tomatoes, peeled
and chopped (or 1
cup canned
tomatoes) ·
4 serrano chiles, or
any variety red or
green hot peppers,
chopped ·
4 tablespoons olive
oil · 1 tablespoon
white vinegar ·
1/2 teaspoon
oregano ·
1/2 teaspoon salt ·
1/4 teaspoon black
pepper · 1 onion,
sliced · 1 avocado,
sliced ·

Cut the fish in serving pieces. Place in a shallow glass casserole dish; sprinkle the juice of five lemons over the fish. Marinate for three hours at room temperature, turning the fish often.

Make a sauce by mixing the tomatoes, chiles or peppers, oil, vinegar, oregano, salt, and pepper. After the fish has marinated for three hours, add the sauce and refrigerate overnight. Serve very cold garnished with slices of onion and avocado.

SERVES 8.

Pescado en Salsa al Minuto

Fish in Minute Sauce

2 pounds bass, haddock, or perch · 1/4 cup water · 1 cup white vinegar · 1/2 teaspoon dried oregano · 2 medium-sized tomatoes, peeled and chopped · 1 large onion, chopped · 1/2 cup olive oil · 4 dried chiles, or any variety red or green hot peppers, chopped · 3 garlic cloves, chopped · 2 hard-boiled eggs, peeled and sliced lengthwise · 20 pimiento-stuffed olives · lettuce ·

Cut the fish in serving pieces. Cook in water, vinegar, and oregano over medium heat about fifteen minutes. Fish should be firm. Place the fish in a shallow casserole dish.

Mix tomatoes, onion, oil, chiles, and garlic together. Pour over the fish and refrigerate overnight. To serve, place on a platter and garnish with eggs, olives, and tender leaves of lettuce.

SERVES 8.

Huachinango al Horno

Baked Red Snapper

1 2-pound red snapper, whole · 1/2 teaspoon salt · 1/4 teaspoon pepper · 2 medium-sized onions, sliced · 4 carrots, scraped and diced · 2 tablespoons white vinegar · 1/4 cup olive oil · 1 bay leaf · 2 lemons, sliced ·

Clean the whole red snapper and give it a few pierces with a fork in order that the juices of the vegetables will penetrate it well; salt and pepper the fish.

Preheat the oven to 325°. Put the whole fish in a shallow baking dish. Cover the fish with onions, carrots, vinegar, oil, and add one bay leaf. Bake about 30 minutes or until the carrots are tender. Remove the bay leaf. Place the fish, carrots, and onion on a platter. Garnish with lemon slices and serve immediately.

SERVES 6.

Filets de Huachinango con Mahonesa

Red Snapper Filets with Mayonnaise

1 2-pound red snapper · 1/2 teaspoon salt · 1/4 teaspoon pepper · 1 tablespoon dehydrated parsley flakes · 1/4 cup olive oil · 10 large pimiento-stuffed olives, sliced · mayonnaise (commercial or home-made) · 3 parsley sprigs ·

Boil the fish in enough water to cover, with salt, pepper, and parsley, for 10 minutes. Remove from the water; drain on paper towels; remove the bones and cut into serving pieces.

Preheat oven to 325°. Arrange the filets in a shallow baking dish greased with olive oil. Pour the remaining oil over the fish. Bake in the middle of the oven for 30 minutes or until the fish is lightly browned.

Serve the fish hot, covered with a thin coating of mayonnaise topped with slices of olives. Garnish the platter with sprigs of parsley.

SERVES 6.

Huachinango a la Marinera

Seaman's Red Snapper

1 2-pound red snapper · 1/2 cup vegetable or olive oil · 2 tablespoons butter · 1/2 medium-sized onion, chopped · 1 parsley sprig, chopped fine · 1 garlic clove, minced · 2 large tomatoes, peeled and chopped · 1 cup sherry wine · 1/2 teaspoon salt · 1/4 teaspoon pepper ·

Wash the fish. Place in a greased casserole dish and set aside.

Melt the oil and butter in a large frying pan. When the grease is hot, add the onion, parsley, garlic, and tomatoes. Fry until the onion is soft. Add sherry, salt and pepper.

Preheat oven to 325°. Cover the fish with the ingredients from the frying pan. Put in casserole dish and cover with foil. Bake for 30 minutes until the fish is tender but not falling from the bone. Serve hot, topped with the sauce.

SERVES 6.

Huachinango a la Veracruz

Veracruz-Style Red Snapper

1 pound filets of red snapper · juice of 1 lemon · 2 tablespoons vegetable oil · 1/2 cup onion, chopped · 2 garlic cloves, minced · 1 16 ounce can tomatoes, drained · 3 tablespoons parsley, chopped · 1 tablespoon vinegar · 1 teaspoon salt · 1 bay leaf · 1/4 teaspoon thyme · 1/4 teaspoon marjoram · 1/4 teaspoon oregano · 1 teaspoon sugar · 1/4 cup water · 9 pimiento-stuffed green olives, sliced · 2 teaspoons capers · 1 canned green chile, chopped · 2 tablespoons olive oil ·

Rub the fish with lemon; sprinkle with salt and pepper. Fry one minute on each side in hot oil; remove to a baking dish. Sauté the onion, garlic, and tomatoes in the remaining oil for five minutes; add next 9 ingredients; cook two minutes more.

Top fish with olives, capers, and chopped chile; pour sauce over all; sprinkle with oil, and bake in a 300° oven until fish flakes apart (about 30 minutes). Do not overcook.

SERVES 4.

Robalo en Salsa Verde

Bass in Green Sauce

2 pounds bass filets · 3 garlic cloves, minced · 1/2 cup vegetable or olive oil · 2 cups canned green sweet English peas · 2 tablespoons parsley, chopped · 1/2 teaspoon salt · 1/4 teaspoon black pepper ·

Brown the garlic and fish in the oil. Remove fish and garlic, and all but about two tablespoons of oil. Add the peas, parsley, salt, and pepper. Simmer about 10 minutes to season. Pour sauce over the filets and serve hot.

SERVES 6.

Pescado en Salsa Colorada

Fish in Red Sauce

2 pounds whole bass · 1/2 cup vinegar · 1/2 teaspoon salt · 6 ancho chiles (large, mild, dark red), or substitute 2 large bell peppers · 2 onions, quartered

15 pimiento-stuffed olivers · parsley ·

Clean the fish. Place in a shallow ovenproof dish. Sprinkle with vinegar, olive oil, and salt. Bake at 400° about 20 minutes.

Devein the chiles and soak them for 30 minutes (unless you are using bell peppers). Fry the chiles or peppers and the onions in three tablespoons of oil until the onion browns.

Place the whole fish on a platter. Top with the onion mixture. Garnish the platter with olives and parsley.

SERVES 6.

Robalitos al Horno

Baked Bass

4 one-pound bass ·
1/2 cup olive oil ·
4 tomatoes, peeled
and chopped ·
3 medium-sized
onions, chopped ·
2 tablespoons
parsley ·
2 tablespoons
vinegar ·
1/2 teaspoon salt ·
1/4 teaspoon
pepper ·

Clean the bass. Place in a shallow ovenproof dish and marinate them one hour at room temperature in the oil, tomatoes, onions, parsley, vinegar, salt and pepper.

Cook in a 400° oven with the marinade, allowing 10 minutes cooking time for each pound of fish.

SERVES 8.

Pescado Nacional

National Fish

2 pounds fish filets,
any variety ·
2 teaspoons salt ·
1/4 teaspoon
pepper · 1 or 2
tablespoons flour ·
1 cup vegetable oil
· 1 small onion,
chopped · 1 garlic
clove ·

Wash the filets and dry them with paper towels. Roll them in a mixture of flour, salt, and pepper.

Heat the oil in a large skillet. Brown the onion and garlic clove to flavor the oil; remove. Fry the filets in the oil over medium heat. Do not crowd in the pan. Brown on one side; turn fish and brown on other side. Drain on paper towels. Serve very hot.

SERVES 6.

Pescadillos con Salsa a la Vinagreta

Small Fish with Vinegar Sauce

2 pounds salt mackerel · 1 cup water · 2 bay leaves · 1/4 teaspoon oregano · 4 garlic cloves, whole · 2 tablespoons olive oil · 3/4 cup white vinegar ·

Clean the mackerel and cover with water. Refrigerate in the water eight hours or more before using. Drain on paper towels.

Simmer the fish in water, to which the bay leaves, oregano, and garlic have been added, for 10 minutes. Drain. Remove bay leaves and garlic.

Preheat oven to 400°. Place the fish in a greased shallow glass baking dish. Sprinkle the fish with oil, and add the vinegar. Bake 20 minutes and serve hot.

SERVES 6.

Bagre en Salsa de Jitomate

Catfish in Tomato Sauce

2 pounds catfish steaks, or small whole catfish · 1/2 cup white flour · 1 cup vegetable oil · 2 tomatoes, peeled and chopped · 1 garlic clove, chopped · 1 tablespoon butter · 1 tablespoon olive oil · 1/2 teaspoon salt · 1/4 teaspoon pepper ·

Flour the fish and brown them in hot oil in a frying pan. Drain.

Prepare the sauce by simmering the tomatoes, garlic, butter, oil, salt, and pepper together for 30 minutes.

Place the fish on a platter and pour the sauce over the fish. Serve hot.

SERVES 6.

Pescado en Todojunto

Fish in "Altogether" Sauce

2 pounds fish filets · 1/4 cup flour · 2 lemons · 1/2 teaspoon salt · 2 tomatoes, peeled and chopped · 2 onions, chopped · 3 garlic cloves, chopped · 3 canned green chiles, chopped · 2 tablespoons butter · 1/4 teaspoon black pepper · 12 pimiento-stuffed olives, sliced ·

Arrange filets side by side in a greased and floured baking dish. Put the filets on top of the flour. Sprinkle them with the juice of two lemons and the salt. Marinate the fish at room temperature in the seasoning while preparing the sauce.

Fry the tomatoes, onions, garlic, and chiles in the butter until the tomatoes and onions are soft.

Pour the sauce over the tomatoes and add black pepper. Bake at 400° for 30 minutes or until the sauce thickens. Garnish each filet with olive slices.

SERVES 6.

Bacalao en Cebollado

Codfish in Onion

1 pound salt codfish · 1/2 cup olive oil · 4 medium-sized onions, sliced · 4 garlic cloves, crushed · 1/4 teaspoon black pepper · pimiento-stuffed olives · capers · parsley ·

Use frozen codfish, following the directions on the package; or, for fresh codfish, cover with cold water overnight or for at least eight hours. Drain. In 1/4 cup of oil, brown the codfish over medium heat. Set aside. Add the rest of the oil to the frying pan and simmer the onions, crushed garlic, and pepper until the onions are soft. Return the fish to the pan. Spoon some of the onions over the fish, cover, and simmer about thirty minutes until the fish feels firm to the touch.

Serve on a platter garnished with olives, capers, and parsley.

SERVES ABOUT 8.

116

Vegetable soup (recipe, page 32). In the finer homes in Mexico, soup is always served from a tureen.

Green Rice (recipe, page 47). A very popular dry soup in Mexico. (RIGHT). Catalan Rice (recipe, page 61) (BELOW).

Tomatoes stuffed with cheese (recipe, page 203)
(BELOW). Fish filets (recipe, page 110) (RIGHT).
Covered chicken (recipe, page 167) (BOTTOM).

Meatballs (recipe, page 137)
(ABOVE). Bakers shoulder of lamb
(recipe, page 152) (LEFT). Eggs with
shrimp make a nice canape (recipe,
page 5) (BELOW).

Guacamole or the avocado salad is a favorite in all of Mexico. It is served with soft tortillas, although crispy tacos are more popular in the United States (recipe, page 207) (LEFT). Rolled enchiladas (recipe, page 85).

These appetizers and canapes are easy to make or you can buy prepared ones in the supermarkets in Mexico. They will be called entremeses. Pictured are olives, tuna, pickles, and peas canned in oil, all attractively surrounded by bright red peppers. Serve with crackers (RIGHT).

(BELOW FROM LEFT TO RIGHT): Rolled Enchiladas (recipe, page 85); Green Tomato Sauce (recipe, page 66); Soft Tortillas, refried beans, and tamales. If you plan to go native, cover a soft tortilla with the sauce and roll the tortilla before eating.

Bacalao en Salsa Roja

Codfish in Red Sauce

2 pounds salt codfish · 1/2 cup olive oil · 4 tablespoons white flour · 2 tomatoes, peeled and chopped · 2 garlic cloves, chopped · 1/4 cup white vinegar · 1/4 teaspoon red pepper · parsley ·

Cover codfish with cold water for eight hours or overnight. Drain. If you are using frozen codfish, follow the directions on the package. They probably will not requiring soaking. Cut the codfish into serving pieces. Heat the oil until moderately hot but not smoking. Dip the pieces of fish in flour and fry until browned, turning to brown on both sides. Drain on paper towels and place on a platter.

Prepare the sauce by simmering the tomatoes, garlic, vinegar, and pepper together for fifteen minutes. Pour the sauce over the fish and serve hot. Garnish the platter with parsley.

SERVES 7–10.

Cherna a la Guintana Roo

Guintana Roo-Style Perch

2 pounds white
perch filets ·
1/2 teaspoon salt ·
2 limes ·
2 tomatoes, peeled
and chopped ·
1 medium-sized
onion, chopped ·
6 garlic cloves,
chopped ·
1/4 teaspoon
ground cumin ·
1/2 teaspoon
oregano ·
1/4 teaspoon black
pepper ·
2 tablespoons
vinegar · 12 large
pimiento-stuffed
olives · parsley ·

Sprinkle the filets with salt, and marinate the perch in the juice of two limes. Mix together with tomatoes, onions, garlic, cumin, oregano, pepper, and vinegar.

Place the fish in a greased pan. Cover with the sauce. Cover the pan and simmer on top of the stove about fifteen minutes until the fish is tender and the sauce is nearly dry. Serve on a platter garnished with olives and sprigs of parsley.

SERVES 6.

Pescado a la Veracruzana

Veracruz-Style Fish

2 pounds fish filets
(haddock or cod) ·
1/2 teaspoon salt ·
2 lemons · 1/2 cup
olive oil ·
2 medium-sized
onions, chopped ·
2 garlic cloves ·
2 cups canned
tomatoes, drained
(or 2 cups tomato
sauce) · 6 jalapeño
peppers, finely
chopped ·
1/4 teaspoon black
pepper · 1/2 cup
water · 18
pimiento-stuffed
olives ·

Sprinkle the filets with salt, and marinate the fish in the juice of two lemons. Heat 1/4 cup of olive oil and fry onion and garlic until the onion is tender. Add the tomatoes or tomato sauce, jalapeños, and pepper. Simmer and add water if the sauce seems too thick.

In another frying pan, heat the remaining 1/4 cup of olive oil, and fry the filets. Add the filets to the sauce mixture and simmer for five minutes. Serve hot, using the olives for garnish.

SERVES 6.

119

Mojarras Rellenas y Empapeladas

Stuffed Sea Fish Wrapped in Paper

4 one-pound whole fish (mackerel, cod, haddock) · 3 lemons · 2 tablespoons salt · 1/4 cup vegetable or olive oil · 1 medium-sized onion, chopped · 1 potato, boiled and chopped · 1 garlic clove, minced · 1/4 cup almonds, blanched and chopped · 1/2 teaspoon salt · 1/4 teaspoon pepper · 2 hard-boiled eggs, chopped ·

Clean the fish and slit lengthwise for stuffing, but do not cut in two pieces. Soak for 15 minutes, in enough water to cover, with the juice of three lemons and salt. Dry on paper towels.

Heat the oil in a frying pan and fry the onion, potato, garlic, almonds, parsley, salt, and pepper until the onion is soft. Mix in the eggs.

Stuff each fish with 1/4 of this mixture. Tie with cord to close. Cover the bottom of a casserole dish with parchment paper or heavy paper (a clean sack will do) which has been heavily greased. Place the fish on top of the paper. Cover with another piece of heavily greased paper. Bake at 350° for about 45 minutes or until the fish can be pulled away from the bone and are moist.

SERVES 6–8.

Pámpano Asado

Broiled Fish

2 pounds fish filets (any variety) · 3 tablespoons lemon juice · 2 teaspoons salt · 2 tablespoons vegetable or olive oil · 4 garlic cloves, minced · 1/4 teaspoon paprika · parsley ·

Soak filets for 15 minutes in water to cover with one tablespoon of lemon juice and one teaspoon of salt. Dry on paper towels.

Cover the broiler with foil which has been greased with vegetable or olive oil. Place the filets on the broiler pan skin side down, if the skin has not been removed. Sprinkle the filets with the remaining lemon juice, vegetable or olive oil, minced garlic, the remaining teaspoon of salt, and paprika.

Place two inches from the heat. Broil 10 or 15 minutes until the filets are brown and will flake easily in the thickest part of the fish. Serve on a platter garnished with parsley.

SERVES 6.

Anillo de Atún

Tuna Ring

2 6-1/2 ounce cans tuna in oil · 1/2 cup soft bread crumbs · 1/4 cup onions, chopped · 1 tablespoon parsley, chopped · 1 teaspoon salt · 1/4 teaspoon pepper · 1 lemon · 2 eggs, slightly beaten · mayonnaise ·

Mix together the tuna, bread crumbs, onions, parsley, salt, pepper, juice of one lemon, and eggs. Place in a greased ring mold.

Preheat oven to 350°. Bake about 45 minutes.

Unmold onto a hot round platter. Fill center with mayonnaise (either commercial or home-made). Serve immediately.

SERVES 6.

Croquetas de Salmón

Salmon Croquettes

2 cups canned salmon · 2-1/2 ounce can of mushroom stems and pieces, drained · 1 cup white sauce · 4 tablespoons onions, chopped · 1 egg, slightly beaten · 1 cup bread crumbs · 1/2 teaspoon salt · 1/4 teaspoon pepper · oil for frying ·

Combine the salmon, mushrooms, sauce, onions, egg, bread crumbs, salt, and pepper. Refrigerate until cold. Shape into croquettes.

Beat another egg with one tablespoon of water. Have ready two dishes of bread or cracker crumbs. Heat the oil slowly; it should be hot but not smoking. Dip each croquette in crumbs, then in egg, then in crumbs again. Fry in the deep fat until a golden brown. Drain on paper towels and serve hot.

SERVES 6.

Conchas a la Gran Duquesa

Grand Duchess-Style Shellfish

2 cups cooked lobster meat, chopped · 1 cup canned crab meat, chopped · 1/2 stick (4 ounces) butter · 2 garlic cloves, chopped · 1 medium-sized onion, chopped · 1 teaspoon salt · 1/2 teaspoon black pepper · 1/2 cup dry white wine · 1/2 cup sharp cheddar cheese, grated ·

Mix the lobster and crab meat together. Set aside.

Melt the butter and cook the garlic and onion seasoned with salt and pepper, until the onion is soft. Add the wine. Remove from the heat. In six oven-proof molds, aluminum foil shells, or crab shells, place a heaping tablespoon of sauce, then add a portion of the lobster and crab meat, then more sauce, until all the mixture is used. Top each shell with cheese. Bake in a moderate oven (375°) 20 minutes or until browned.

SERVES 6.

Jaibas Rellenas

Stuffed Crab

12 crabs, or
substitute 3 cups
canned crab meat ·
2 tablespoons olive
oil · 2 tablespoons
parsley, chopped ·
2 medium-sized
tomatoes, peeled
and chopped ·
1 onion, finely
chopped · 2 garlic
cloves, chopped ·
1 tablespoon white
vinegar · 8
pimiento-stuffed
olives, chopped ·
1/2 teaspoon salt ·
1/4 teaspoon black
pepper · 3/4 cup
bread crumbs ·
4 tablespoons
butter · paprika ·

Boil the live crabs in enough salted water to cover them; cover and cook 15 to 20 minutes until the crabs become very red. Remove from the water and allow to cool.

Split the shells and remove the meat. Save the shells.

Prepare a sauce by frying parsley, tomatoes, onion, garlic, vinegar, olives, salt, ground pepper, and the crab meat into the oil for five minutes. Place this mixture into the crab shells or into 12 small aluminum foil shells. Cover each shell with bread crumbs, butter, and a dash of paprika. Bake in a moderate oven (375°) 20 minutes or until browned.

SERVES 6.

Roe frequently will be found in fresh fish caught in the spring. Some of the most common sources of roe are salmon, cod, haddock, flounder, herring, and mackerel. It may be bought by the pound in fish markets or by the can in supermarkets.

To prepare roe for the following two recipes, place one pound of roe in one quart of boiling water to which two tablespoons of lemon juice have been added. Simmer 10 minutes. Drain and cool. Remove membrane from each roe.

Tortitas de Hueva

Roe Patties

1 pound roe ·
4 tomatoes, peeled
and chopped ·
1 medium-sized
onion, chopped ·
2 garlic cloves,
chopped · 2 eggs,
beaten ·
1 teaspoon salt ·
parsley ·

Prepare the roe according to the preceding directions for "Fish Roe." Mash immediately. Mix with tomatoes, onions, garlic, eggs, and salt.

Pat out the mixture into 12 round patties about one inch thick and three inches around. Place the cakes in a greased baking dish; bake in a 350° oven for 30 minutes. Place on a platter and garnish with sprigs of parsley.

SERVES 6.

Tortillas de Hueva

Roe Omelet

1 pound roe ·
2 tomatoes, peeled
and chopped ·
1 medium-sized
onion, chopped ·
2 garlic cloves,
chopped ·
1 teaspoon
chopped parsley ·
2 small jalapeño
chiles · 1 teaspoon
salt · 1/4 teaspoon
black pepper ·
1/2 cup dry white
wine · 4 eggs,
beaten ·

Prepare the roe according to the directions for "Fish Roe." Let the roe dry; then mash them firmly. Add to the tomatoes, onion, garlic, parsley, chiles, salt, and pepper. Beat the eggs with the wine and add to the vegetables and roe. Place in a greased baking dish; cook at 350° for 30 minutes until the eggs are dry.

SERVES 6.

Shrimp is a sea food enjoyed all over Mexico.

To prepare two pounds of fresh shrimp, bring one quart of water, to which has been added one stalk of celery with leaves, three or four slices of onion, and three thin slices of lemon to a boil. Add the fresh shrimp; bring to a second boil; turn off heat and let stand in the hot water for six to eight minutes. The shrimp should be pink when they are tender. Drain. You may want to reserve the liquid for fish broth. Remove the shells and refrigerate. Two pounds serves 6.

Camarones en Frío

Cold Shrimp

2 pounds fresh or frozen shrimp · 3 large onions, 2 sliced and 1 chopped fine · 3 lemons · 1/2 cup vegetable or olive oil · 3 garlic cloves, chopped · 3 large tomatoes, peeled and chopped · 1/2 cup white vinegar · 1 8-ounce can jalapeño peppers · 1/2 teaspoon dry mustard · 1 tablespoon salt · 1/4 teaspoon black pepper ·

Prepare the fresh shrimp according to the preceding directions for "Fresh Shrimp." If you are using frozen shrimp, prepare according to the instructions on the package, but add the celery, onion, and lemon slices to the boiling water. Refrigerate the shrimp.

Marinate two onions in the juice of three lemons and a pinch of salt for two hours before serving.

Heat the oil on the stove and add the other onion, (chopped fine) the garlic, tomatoes, vinegar, the can of Jalapeños and their liquid (reserving 3 of the Jalapeños for garnish), mustard, salt, and pepper. Cook about 15 minutes until the onion is soft. Cool before serving.

Serve the shrimp cold topped with the sauce and garnish with the marinated onions and Jalapeños cut in strips.

SERVES 6.

Camarones Fritos

Fried Shrimp

2 pounds fresh or frozen shrimp · 1/2 cup vinegar · 1/2 teaspoon black pepper · 1 cup vegetable or olive oil · 4 garlic cloves · lemon wedges ·

Prepare the fresh shrimp according to the preceding directions for "Fresh Shrimp." If you are using frozen shrimp, prepare according to the instructions on the package, but add the celery, onion, and lemon slices to the boiling water. Peel but do not refrigerate.

Marinate the shrimp in vinegar and black pepper for 30 minutes.

Brown the garlic in the oil (about 370°). Remove. Fry the shrimp in the same oil until they begin to swell. Do not crowd in the frying pan. Drain on a paper towel, and serve hot with wedges of lemon.

SERVES 6.

Just as the coastal towns in Mexico are noted for their shrimp, they are equally renowned for their fresh oysters. Not only do the coastal areas feature their oyster bars, but many of the inland towns and cities do also. As in all the cuisine of the country, the Mexicans add their own flare to the preparation and serving of oysters.

To prepare oysters that are still in the shell, scrub the shells thoroughly and rinse under cold water. Insert a strong knife into the unhinged side of the oyster shell, and cut through the muscle which holds the two halves. If you plan to save the juice, open the oysters over a bowl.

If you are not one of those who has the knack of opening oysters this way, place the unopened oysters in a preheated hot oven (400°–425°) for about six minutes. Remove them from the oven and put them in cold water for a minute or two. Drain and proceed by inserting the knife into the unhinged side. This time, they should open easily. Save the shells. They can be used for oyster recipes and for other sea foods as well. Allow 6 oysters for each serving.

Ostiones en su Concha

Oysters in Their Shell

12 raw oysters ·
2 tablespoons
butter · 1 garlic
clove · juice of 1/2
lemon ·
1 tablespoon
parsley, minced ·
1/4 teaspoon salt ·
a few grains of
black pepper ·

Prepare the oysters following the directions for "Fresh Oysters." Reserve 12 shells. Rub the shells in garlic for flavor and grease each shell with butter. Place an oyster in each shell.

Preheat the oven to 350°. Place the oysters in their shells on a cookie sheet, and bake several minutes until the edges of the oysters begin to curl. Remove from the oven and top each oyster with a sauce made by combining the remaining butter (melted), lemon juice, parsley, salt, and pepper. Serve in the shells.

SERVES 2.

Ostiones en Escabeche

Pickled Oysters

2 dozen oysters ·
1/4 cup water ·
juice of 1 lemon ·
1/2 teaspoon salt ·
4 tablespoons
vinegar · 2 large
onions, chopped ·
2 garlic cloves,
minced ·
1/2 4-ounce can
jalapeño chiles,
chopped ·

Prepare the oysters following the directions for "Fresh Oysters." Save 24 shells. Simmer the oysters in the water, lemon juice, and salt for two minutes or until the oysters are plump. Remove from the heat and drain well. Simmer the vinegar, onions, garlic, Jalapeños, and the oyster liquid for 15 minutes. Pour the sauce over the oysters and refrigerate at least 24 hours. Serve cold in oyster shells.

SERVES 4.

Ostiones a la Marinera

Marine Oysters

2 dozen fresh oysters, or 1 pint of already opened oysters · 1/4 cup vegetable or olive oil · 5 garlic cloves, chopped · 2 medium-sized onions, chopped · 2 tomatoes, peeled and chopped · 1 teaspoon salt · 1/2 teaspoon black pepper · 1 cup dry red wine ·

Prepare the oysters following the directions for "Fresh Oysters," or substitute one pint of already opened oysters, which may be found in the meat department of most supermarkets.

Heat the oil in a frying pan until hot but not burning. Add the finely chopped garlic and onions. When they begin to brown, add tomatoes, salt, pepper, the oysters, and their liquid. Lower the fire and simmer for 15 minutes. Add wine; simmer 10 more minutes tightly covered. Serve hot with white rice.

SERVES 4–5.

la carne

9

meat

Meats, which are so popular in today's Mexico, were not known in Montezuma's court, where the main dishes had been sea, poultry, and game food. It was the Spanish who brought the domesticated animals to the country: the Indians of Mexico had never seen a horse until Cortés and his conquerors invaded the land. In fact, we can credit the horse with helping to conquer the country. The Indians were so in awe of these armored "beings" on horseback that they believed horse and man were one—a strange, four-legged "god," whom they feared.

The popular varieties of meat in Mexico today are the same as in the United States—beef, veal, pork, and lamb—enjoyed primarily by the middle or wealthier classes. Meat is a rarity among the poorer class, a luxury reserved for fiestas. As with all the cuisine of the country, the Mexicans add their own gusto to the preparation of meats.

Chorizo Hecho en Casa

Homemade Link Chorizo Sausage

Chorizo sausage appears in many of the recipes. Although you can prepare this at home, if you live in an area which sells chorizos, I recommend that you buy them at the store.

sausage casings (enough for 20 4-inch sausages), available at meat packing suppliers · 1-1/2 cups vinegar · 2 pounds pork · 1-1/4 cups pork or beef fat · 2 large onions, chopped · 6 garlic cloves, chopped · 1 4-ounce can pimientos · 1/4 cup brandy or tequila · 1-1/2 teaspoons salt · 1 teaspoon cinnamon · 1 teaspoon ground black pepper · 2 tablespoons chili powder ·

After soaking the casings in warm water for four hours, put one end of the casing over the end of the water faucet and run water through it. Pour a cup of vinegar through the casings in order that the sausage will keep better.

Grind the pork, chop the fat finely, and add the onion, garlic, pimientos, 1/2 cup of vinegar, brandy or tequila, salt, and spices. Season with chili powder and mix well.

Cut the casings in four-foot lengths in order to stuff more easily. Tie one end and remove air from length by pressing toward the open end; fill with the mixture using a funnel, a cake decorator, or a sausage machine. Tie every four inches.

Hang the links outdoors to dry for a day. If refrigerated and the casing is not cut open, they will keep for several weeks.

MAKES 20 SAUSAGES.

Chicharrón en Chile Verde

Thick, Crisp Bacon in Green Sauce

1 pound thick bacon · 6 small green tomatoes, chopped · 4 or 5 mountain chiles, chopped, or substitute any variety of small green hot chile pepper · 2 tablespoons water · 1 small onion, chopped · 1/4 teaspoon ground coriander · 1 garlic clove, chopped · 1 tablespoon olive oil ·

Fry the bacon crisp, and drain on paper towels.

Cook the tomatoes and chiles in a little water until the tomatoes are soft. Add the onion, garlic, coriander, olive oil, and bacon (which has been crumbled). Simmer for five minutes. If the mixture thickens too much, add a little water.

Serve with eggs for brunch or with white rice for an evening meal.

SERVES 6.

Bisteques Rusos

Russian Beefsteaks

1 pound ground chuck · 1/4 teaspoon nutmeg · 1/2 teaspoon salt · 1/4 teaspoon pepper · 2 tablespoons flour · 4 tablespoons vegetable or olive oil · 4 eggs ·

Season the meat with nutmeg, salt, and pepper. Divide in four equal sections; then flatten these until they are about 1/4 inch thick—like a hamburger. Roll them in flour and fry in oil, turning once, until they are brown on both sides. Cook them longer if you want them well-done. Drain on paper towels.

Fry the eggs in the leftover grease; season with salt and pepper and serve over the ground beefsteaks.

SERVES 4.

Bisteques a la americana

American-Style Beefsteaks

4 filet mignon or sirloin beefsteaks (1-1/2 inches thick) · 3 tablespoons vegetable or olive oil · 4 eggs · 4 pieces white toast, crusts removed · butter · lemon juice · salt ·

Pan broil the steaks to your liking (rare, medium, well-done) in a little oil. Charcoaled meat has become popular in Mexico; so you may prefer to prepare your steaks charcoal broiled.

In another frying pan, add oil and fry the eggs. Toast four pieces of bread and butter them while they are hot. Top each piece of toast with a steak, a few drops of lemon juice, an egg, and salt to taste.

SERVES 4.

Bisteques con Anchoas

Beefsteak with Anchovies

4 sirloin beefsteaks · 1 tablespoon olive oil · 2 garlic cloves, chopped · 2 tablespoons parsley, chopped · 4 rolled anchovies, canned ·

Sear the steaks in a frying pan on both sides in oil. Add the garlic and parsley and a little more oil, if necessary. Simmer with the steaks for ten minutes. Before serving, top each steak with an anchovy.

SERVES 4.

Filetes de Res a la Gallega

Galician-Style Beef Filets

8 beef filets, 1-1/2 inches thick · 2 eggs, beaten · 1 cup milk · 1/2 teaspoon salt · bread crumbs · 3 tablespoons olive oil · 1 lemon, sliced ·

Marinate the filets at room temperature with eggs, milk, and salt for two or three hours.

Dip the filets in bread crumbs and pan broil in the oil about one minute on each side. If you prefer your steaks well-done, cook them longer, but the cooking time will not need to be as long because of the marinating. Serve on a platter garnished with slices of lemon.

SERVES 8.

Solomillo de Buey "Regencia"

Regency-Style Beef Sirloin

2 pounds beef roast · 1/4 pound bacon, sliced · 4 carrots, cut thin · 2 onions, sliced · 1 bay leaf · 1 cup dry white wine · 1/2 teaspoon salt · 4 ounce can whole mushrooms · 1 tablespoon butter ·

Put the roast in a shallow uncovered roasting pan. Place the strips of bacon over the roast. Add carrots, onions, bay leaf, wine, and salt.

Bake in a 300° oven, allowing 45 minutes for rare and one hour for medium-rare meat.

Simmer the mushrooms in butter. Place the meat, carrots, onions, and mushrooms on a platter. Strain the sauce from the meat and serve separately in a gravy bowl.

SERVES 4.

Albondigas

Meat Balls

1 pound ground beef · 1/2 pound ground pork · 1 cup cooked ham, ground · 1 cup bread crumbs, fine · 1 medium-sized onion, grated · 1 garlic clove, chopped · 1/2 teaspoon coriander · 1 teaspoon parsley, chopped · 1 teaspoon salt · 1/2 teaspoon black pepper · 2 eggs, beaten · 3 tablespoons vegetable oil · 2 medium tomatoes, peeled and mashed · 4 cups broth, beef or vegetable ·

Mix meats with bread crumbs, half the onion, garlic, coriander, parsley, salt, pepper, and eggs. Mold into balls about one inch in diameter.

Heat oil, and sauté the rest of the onion for five minutes. Remove from the pan, and brown the meat balls. Return the onion to the pan, and add the tomatoes and broth. Simmer for one and one-half to two hours.

SERVES 6.

Ternera con Chícaros

Veal with Peas

1 pound veal cutlets · 3 tablespoons vegetable or olive oil · 1 medium-sized tomato, peeled and chopped · 1/2 cup beef broth · bay leaf, small piece · 1/4 teaspoon dried thyme · 2 teaspoons salt · 1/4 teaspoon black pepper · 1 17-ounce can sweet green peas, drained ·

Heat oil in heavy frying pan and brown cutlets on both sides. Add tomato, broth, bay leaf, thyme, salt, and pepper. Cover and simmer fifteen minutes more. After ten minutes, add the can of peas. Remove bay leaf before serving.

SERVES 6.

Filetes de Ternera con Pimientos

Veal Filets with Peppers

4 large veal cutlets · 3 tablespoons butter · 2 teaspoons salt · 2 bell peppers, cut in strips · 1/4 cup water · parsley ·

Salt the cutlets and brown them in butter in a heavy frying pan. Add the peppers and water; simmer until the cutlets are tender.

Place on a platter; top each cutlet with green pepper strips; garnish the platter with sprigs of parsley.

SERVES 4.

Ternera con Berenjenas

Veal with Eggplant

2-1/2 pounds veal cutlets · 3 tablespoons vegetable or olive oil · 3 tablespoons white vinegar · 1 medium-sized onion, chopped · 1 medium-sized tomato, chopped · 2 medium-sized eggplants · 2 teaspoons salt · 1/4 teaspoon black pepper ·

Heat oil and vinegar in heavy frying pan and simmer cutlets for 15 minutes. Set the meat aside. Simmer the onion and tomato in the frying pan (in which the meat has been cooked) for 10 minutes. Return the meat to the pan, and add enough water to cover the pieces.

While the meat is cooking, peel the eggplants and cut in slices the long way. When the meat is tender, add the eggplant, salt, and pepper. Cover and simmer until the eggplant is soft.

SERVES 6–8.

Ternera en Ajillo

Veal in Garlic

2 pounds veal cutlets · 3 tablespoons olive oil · 2 8-ounce size cans tomato sauce · 6 garlic cloves, chopped · 2 teaspoons salt · 1/2 teaspoon black pepper · bread crumbs ·

Brown the cutlets in the oil. Place the meat in a well-greased shallow casserole dish. Add the tomato sauce, garlic, salt, and pepper, and top with bread crumbs.

Cover the casserole and bake in a 325° oven until the meat is tender, about 30 minutes.

SERVES 6–8.

Chuletas de Ternera Mechada

Fried Veal Cutlets

4 veal cutlets ·
3 slices bacon, cut
in 1 inch pieces ·
1 cup dry white
wine ·
2 tablespoons
tomato paste ·
1/2 cup cooked
ham, cubed ·
3 large sweet
peppers, cut in fine
strips · 1/4 cup
water ·
2 teaspoons salt ·
1/4 teaspoon black
pepper · 4 eggs,
hard-boiled and
sliced ·

Brown the cutlets with the bacon. Add the wine, tomato paste, ham, peppers, water, salt, and pepper. Cover and simmer 30 minutes, or until the veal is tender.

Place on a platter, and garnish with slices of hard-boiled eggs.

SERVES 4.

140

Ternera Mechada con Jamón

Veal Cutlet with Ham

1-1/2 pounds veal cutlets, 1/4 inch thick · 3 slices bacon, cut in 1-inch pieces · 1 medium-sized onion, chopped · 1/2 cup cooked ham, diced · 1/4 cup flour · 3 tablespoons vegetable or olive oil · 1 cup dry white wine · 1/2 cup warm water · 2 small bay leaves · 1/2 teaspoon salt · 1/4 teaspoon pepper ·

Cut the veal in six pieces; pound to 1/4 inch thickness with a meat pounder or with the edge of a heavy plate.

Saute the onion with the bacon in a large heavy skillet until the onion is soft. On each cutlet place some of the bacon and onion mixture, and some cooked ham. Roll up meat and fasten each piece with toothpicks or tie with string. Roll each cutlet in flour.

Add oil to the same skillet in which the onion and bacon were cooked. Brown the cutlets over medium heat; then add wine, water, bay leaves, salt, and pepper. Cover and simmer for 45 minutes, or until meat is tender.

SERVES 6.

Carne Guisada a la Moderna

Modern-Style Roast

1-1/2 pounds veal shoulder, tied, boned and rolled · 2 tablespoons vegetable oil · 2 medium-sized onions, sliced · 1/2 pound fresh mushrooms · 1 6-ounce can ripe olives, unpitted · 1/2 teaspoon sugar · 1/2 teaspoon salt · 1/4 teaspoon pepper · 8-10 small whole potatoes, peeled ·

Brown the meat in the oil.

Grease a casserole dish generously and line it with the onion, mushrooms, and olives. Add the meat, sugar, salt, and pepper; put the potatoes around the meat.

Cover the casserole dish and bake in a slow oven (325°) for two hours or until the meat is tender.

Serve the meat on a large platter garnished with olives, mushrooms, and potatoes.

SERVES 6.

Higado de Ternera con Champiñones

Calves Liver with Mushrooms

1-1/2 pounds calves liver · 1/2 pound fresh mushrooms, sliced · 2 garlic cloves, chopped · 1 sprig parsley, chopped · 1 tablespoon butter · 2 tablespoons vegetable oil · parsley for garnish · 1 teaspoon salt · 1/2 teaspoon pepper ·

Wash liver and set aside to dry. Sauté the mushrooms, garlic and parsley in a frying pan in butter for 10 minutes. Season with salt and pepper; add a few drops of water if the mixture begins to dry.

In another frying pan, heat the oil and fry the liver quickly for tenderness, about three minutes on each side.

Serve the liver on a platter, covered with the mushrooms; garnish with parsley.

SERVES 6.

Higado Guisado con Salsa

Liver Cooked with Sauce

1-1/2 pounds calves liver · 1/4 cup butter · 4 medium-sized tomatoes, peeled and chopped · 1 garlic clove, chopped · 1 medium-sized onion, chopped · 1 sprig parsley, chopped · 4 medium-sized potatoes, sliced · 1 teaspoon salt · 1/4 teaspoon pepper · 1/2 cup beef broth ·

Brown liver in butter quickly, about three minutes on each side. Remove from pan, but keep warm. In the same pan, sauté tomatoes, garlic, onion, parsley, and potatoes. Season with salt and pepper. Add the broth and simmer until the potatoes are tender.

Serve the liver on a platter, surrounded with the potatoes, and covered with the tomato sauce.

SERVES 6.

Mochomos

Shredded Pork Meat

1-1/2 pounds pork meat · 2 cups water · 2 tablespoons butter · 1 teaspoon salt ·
For Garnish:
1 ripe tomato, sliced ·
1 medium-sized onion, sliced ·
guacamole salad ·

Cook the meat in the water for 30 or 40 minutes until the water has evaporated. Grind or shred the meat; add salt; fry the meat in the butter until it is a golden brown.

Place the meat in the center of a platter garnished with sliced tomatoes, onions, and guacamole salad (Recipe on page 207).

SERVES 6.

Carne de Cerdo a la Cubana

Cuban-Style Pork

1-1/2 pounds pork meat · 1 cup vinegar · 4 garlic cloves, crushed · 1/2 teaspoon oregano · 1 teaspoon salt · 2 tablespoons vegetable or olive oil, lard, or butter · 4 bananas, (not too ripe) peeled and sliced lengthwise ·

Marinate the pork, cut in strips, in vinegar, garlic, oregano, and salt for one hour at room temperature. Turn the strips of meat several times.

Melt the oil or lard in a heavy skillet. Brown the pork strips evenly on all sides. Lower the heat and cover. Simmer the meat slowly until the meat is tender.

Remove meat to platter. In the same skillet, sauté the bananas until golden brown. Add more oil, lard, or butter to the pan if necessary. Garnish the platter with the fried bananas.

SERVES 6.

Costillas a la Veracruzana

Veracruz-Style Pork Chops

2 pounds pork chops · 4 large tomatoes, peeled and chopped · 4 pasilla chiles, or substitute green pepper · 1 tablespoon vinegar · 1 cup dry cooking sherry · 1 garlic clove, chopped · 1 teaspoon oregano · 1 small bay leaf · 1/2 teaspoon salt · 1/4 teaspoon pepper · 1 cup sour cream ·

Place the pork chops in a slightly greased baking dish. Set aside. Simmer the tomatoes and chiles on top of the stove until the tomatoes are soft. Add vinegar, sherry, garlic, oregano, bay leaf, salt, and pepper to the tomato mixture. Pour this mixture over the pork chops.

Preheat oven to 350°. Bake an hour and a half until the pork chops are tender. 10 minutes before removing the meat from the oven, add the sour cream.

SERVES 6.

Adobo

Pickled Meat

4 pounds pork loin roast · 2 medium-sized onions, chopped · 1 teaspoon salt · 1/4 teaspoon pepper · 1 cup water · 6 ancho chiles, or green peppers, or 3 bell peppers, chopped · 2 tablespoons bacon fat or butter · 2 garlic cloves, chopped · 1/2 teaspoon oregano · 1 small bay leaf · 1/2 cup vinegar ·

Preheat oven to 350°. Bake the roast with one of the onions, salt, pepper, and water for two and a half hours. Pork should always be cooked until well-done.

In a pan, melt the fat and sauté the chiles or peppers. Add the remaining onion, garlic, oregano, bay leaf, and vinegar. Simmer until the onion is soft. Remove the roast from the oven, and put the meat, onion, and pork broth in the pan with the vinegar sauce. Bring to a boil and cover. Lower the fire and simmer 15 minutes. Remove the roast to a platter; pour the sauce over the roast, and serve.

SERVES 8–10.

Lomo de Cerdo Cocido con Leche

Pork Loin Cooked with Milk

2-1/2 pounds pork loin roast · 1 tablespoon shortening · 1 teaspoon salt · 1/4 teaspoon pepper · 3 cups milk ·

Brown the meat on all sides in the shortening. Season with salt and pepper. Add the milk and simmer an hour. The meat should be very tender when pierced with a fork. Stir the dish from time to time to avoid its sticking to the pan.

Remove the meat when it is tender, slice, and cover with the milk sauce to serve.

SERVES 5–6.

Lomo de Cerdo Cocido con Cerveza

Pork Loin Cooked with Beer

2-1/2 pounds pork loin roast · 1 tablespoon shortening · 1 teaspoon salt · 1/4 teaspoon pepper · 2 cups beer ·

Follow the preceding recipe for "Pork Loin Cooked with Milk," substituting two cups of beer for the milk.

SERVES 5–6.

Lomo de Puerco con Vino Blanco

Pork Loin with White Wine

2 pounds pork loin roast · 1 tablespoon shortening · 1 teaspoon salt · 1/4 teaspoon pepper · 1 medium-sized onion, sliced · 1/4 teaspoon oregano · 1/4 teaspoon thyme · 1 small bay leaf · 1 cup dry white wine · 1/2 cup water ·

Grease the roast and a shallow baking dish with the shortening. Place the roast in the baking dish, and season with salt and pepper. Add onion, oregano, thyme, bay leaf, wine, and water. Bake at 350°, allowing 35 to 40 minutes per pound.

Slice before serving and cover with the wine sauce.

SERVES 4.

Puerco al Horno

Baked Pork

4 pounds pork loin roast · 2 cups vinegar · 2 medium-sized onions, sliced · 2 garlic cloves, minced · 4 carrots, scraped and sliced · 1/2 teaspoon dried thyme · 1 small bay leaf · 1 tablespoon shortening · 2 teaspoons salt · 1/2 teaspoon pepper · 2 cups water · 6 large canned green chiles · 1 stick cinnamon or 1/4 teaspoon powdered cinnamon · 1/4 teaspoon nutmeg ·

Marinate the pork with the vinegar, onions, garlic, carrots, thyme, and bay leaf overnight or for at least 12 hours in the refrigerator.

Remove the pork from the marinade and rub it with shortening. Sprinkle with salt and pepper. Place in a shallow baking dish with two cups of water. Cover the meat with foil, and bake in a 350° oven for two and a half hours. After two hours of baking, remove the foil, and place the chiles, the garlic used in the marinade, the cinnamon and nutmeg, and one-half cup of the vinegar used in the marinade over the roast. Baste until the meat browns.

Serve sliced garnished with the marinated onions and carrots.

SERVES 10.

Carne Magra de Cerdo con Jitomate

Pork Loin with Tomato

2 pounds pork loin roast · 1 teaspoon salt · 1 tablespoon shortening or butter · 2 garlic cloves, chopped · 4 large tomatoes, peeled and chopped · 1 small bay leaf · 1/4 teaspoon dried thyme ·

Brown the salted roast in a frying pan on all sides in the shortening. Place meat in shallow baking dish in a 350° oven and bake for one hour and 15 minutes.

Meanwhile, prepare a sauce by browning the garlic in the frying pan in which the pork was browned. Add more shortening if necessary. Lower the heat to simmer; add tomatoes, bay leaf, and thyme. When the mixture begins to thicken, strain it.

Serve the roast sliced and covered with the strained tomato sauce.

SERVES 4–5.

Chuletas de Cordera a la Hortelana

Gardener's Wife Lamb Chops

8 shoulder lamb chops · 4 carrots, scraped and sliced · 2 medium-sized onions, sliced · 1 garlic clove, chopped · 4 medium-sized potatoes, sliced · 1/2 teaspoon salt · 1/4 teaspoon pepper · 2 celery stalks, diced · 1 cup vegetable or meat broth · parsley, finely chopped ·

Brown the chops evenly on both sides in a hot un-greased skillet. Lower the heat and cook 12 minutes if chops are one inch thick, 18 minutes if chops are one and a half inches thick, and 22 minutes for two inch thick chops. Place on a warming platter.

Brown the carrots, onions, garlic, and potatoes in the same skillet. Preheat oven to 350°. Place the chops in a shallow ovenproof casserole dish. Salt and pepper the chops, and cover them with the carrots, onions, garlic, potatoes, celery, and broth. Cover and bake for 30 minutes or until the carrots and potatoes are tender.

Serve on a platter with the vegetables. Garnish the chops with parsley.

SERVES 4.

149

Cordero con Champiñones

Lamb with Mushrooms

8 shoulder lamb chops · 8 small onions, whole · 1 tablespoon flour · 1 garlic clove, chopped · 1/2 cup dry white wine · 1/4 cup meat broth or water · 1/2 teaspoon salt · 1/4 teaspoon pepper · 8 ounce can mushrooms, sliced and drained, or 1/2 pound fresh mushrooms · 2 tablespoons butter · parsley ·

Brown the chops and onions in a skillet over a hot fire. Lower the fire to simmer. Sprinkle the meat with flour; add the garlic clove, wine, broth or water, salt, and pepper. Simmer until the meat is tender.

Sauté the mushrooms in butter. About 20 minutes before serving, add the mushrooms to the meat.

Garnish the serving platter with parsley.

SERVES 4.

Chuletas de Cordero con Jitomates y Acetunas

Lamb Chops with Tomatoes and Olives

4 shoulder lamb chops ·
1 tablespoon vegetable oil ·
1 cup dry white wine ·
2 tablespoons tomato paste ·
2 large ripe tomatoes · 4 large mushroom crowns · butter ·
4 canned round anchovies ·
12 pimiento-stuffed green olives · salt and pepper ·

Brown the chops in oil. Lower the heat and cook 15 minutes. Drain and place on a warming platter.

Pour wine into the skillet in which the chops were cooked. Let it cook down a bit; add the tomato paste, stirring continually until the mixture reaches the consistency of gravy.

Cut the tomatoes in half. Season each half with salt and pepper and sprinkle with a few drops of oil. Bake in a 300° oven until they are soft but not mushy.

Sauté the mushrooms in a little butter.

Put the tomato halves on a round plate. On each half, place a lamb chop garnished with an anchovy and mushroom. Garnish the plate with olives.

Serve the tomato sauce as a side dish in a gravy bowl.

SERVES 4.

Espalda de Cordero a la Panadera

Baker's-Style Lamb Shoulder

4–5 pounds boneless rolled lamb shoulder roast · 1 garlic clove · 1/2 pound sliced bacon · 1 teaspoon salt · 1/2 teaspoon pepper · 4 ounces (1 stick) butter · 2 medium-sized onions, sliced · 16 new potatoes, peeled · 2 tablespoons shortening · 1/2 cup vegetable broth or water · parsley, chopped ·

Remove the lamb from the refrigerator half an hour before roasting.

Rub the meat with the garlic clove, and season with salt and pepper. Put half of the bacon in the bottom of an ovenproof pan; then place the shoulder fat side up on top of the bacon, and cover with the rest of the bacon. Add the butter, and cook in a pre-heated 350° oven for two to two and a half hours, allowing 30 minutes per pound for well-done meat.

Meanwhile, fry the onions and potatoes in a frying pan with shortening until they are a golden brown. After the roast has been cooking for 30 minutes, add the onions, potatoes, and broth or warm water.

Serve the shoulder on a platter with the onions and potatoes. Garnish the meat with parsley.

SERVES 8.

Cordero Asado a la Cazadora

Hunter's-Style Roast Lamb

5–6 pound leg of lamb · 3 garlic cloves, sliced · 1/8 teaspoon red pepper · 1 teaspoon salt · 1/8 teaspoon black pepper · 1 small bay leaf · 1/2 teaspoon oregano · 1 cup water · 2 tablespoons butter · 1 lemon · 1 small tomato, sliced ·

Pierce the skin of the meat and insert slices of garlic. Refrigerate overnight in a pickle sauce made of red pepper, salt, black pepper, bay leaf, oregano, and water.

Remove the lamb from the refrigerator 30 minutes before cooking. Place in a shallow baking dish. Dot with butter and the juice of one lemon, and add the sliced tomato. Bake with the marinade in a 350° oven, allowing 30 minutes per pound for well-done meat. Serve hot.

SERVES 8–10.

Pierna de Cordero con Alcachofas Fritas

Leg of Lamb with Fried Artichokes

4 pound leg of lamb ·
2 tablespoons oil ·
2 garlic cloves, sliced ·
1/2 teaspoon dry thyme · 1 teaspoon salt · 1/4 teaspoon pepper · 1 onion, sliced · 1 bay leaf ·
1 cup dry white wine · 1/2 cup water · 8 artichoke hearts, frozen or canned · 1 lemon ·
3 tablespoons flour · shortening, for deep fat frying ·

Brown the leg of lamb in the oil. Lower the heat; pierce the skin of the meat and insert slices of garlic. Sprinkle the meat with thyme, salt, and pepper. Add the onion, bay leaf, wine, and water. Simmer until the meat is tender, allowing 20 minutes per pound, or an hour and a half for a four pound leg of lamb.

Boil the artichoke hearts in two inches of water, to which the juice of one lemon has been added, until tender, about 15 minutes. Drain. Shake the artichoke hearts in a paper sack with the flour. Set aside for a few minutes before frying. Deep fat fry at 350° until the hearts are a golden brown.

Place the meat on a platter; strain the sauce, and pour it over the meat. Arrange the artichoke hearts around the lamb and serve hot.

SERVES 8.

Pierna de Cordero con Habichuelas

Leg of Lamb with Kidney Beans

4–5 pound leg of lamb · 2 garlic cloves, sliced · 2 tablespoons oil · 1/2 teaspoon dried thyme · 1 teaspoon salt · 1/4 teaspoon pepper · 1 bay leaf · 1 large tomato, peeled and chopped · 1/4 cup warm water · 1 tablespoon bacon fat · 2 tablespoons onion · 2 tablespoons green pepper · 1 number 2 can red kidney beans · 2 teaspoons chili powder · 1 tablespoon worcestershire sauce · 1/4 cup Cheddar cheese, grated ·

Pierce the skin of the leg of lamb and insert slices of garlic. Grease a shallow casserole dish wth oil. Add the lamb sprinkled with thyme, salt, and pepper. Add a bay leaf, tomato, and water. Bake at 300°, allowing 30 minutes per pound, or two hours for a four pound leg. Baste the meat in its juice frequently.

Sauté the onion and green pepper in the bacon fat about five minutes, or until soft but not browned. Stir in the beans, chili powder, and Worcestershire sauce. Heat until very hot.

When the leg of lamb is tender, serve it on a large platter. Strain the sauce from the meat pan and serve it in a gravy bowl. Serve the beans, sprinkled with Cheddar cheese, in a vegetable dish.

SERVES 6.

Estofado de Carnero

Mutton Stew

2 pounds mutton or lamb, sliced thin · 2 tablespoons vegetable oil · 1 cup dry white wine · 1 onion, chopped · 2 small tomatoes, peeled and chopped · 1 green pepper, chopped · 2 garlic cloves, minced · 1 small bay leaf · 1/4 teaspoon dried thyme · 1 teaspoon salt · 1/4 teaspoon black pepper ·

Although this recipe calls for sliced mutton, lamb may be substituted. Mutton meat comes from lambs beyond the age of a year and a half. For this reason the meat is tougher and should be cooked longer.

Brown the mutton or lamb in the oil. Add wine, onion, tomatoes, green pepper, garlic, bay leaf, thyme, salt, and pepper. Simmer an hour or an hour and a half for lamb, and an hour and a half to two hours for mutton. Pierce with a fork for tenderness.

Serve hot, covering the meat with the sauce.

SERVES 4.

Carnero Picante

Spicy Mutton

4 pound leg of lamb or mutton · 1 teaspoon salt · 1/2 teaspoon red pepper · 1/2 pound bacon, sliced · 2 medium-sized onions, sliced · 2 medium-sized tomatoes, peeled and sliced · 1 tablespoon heavy cream · 1/2 teaspoon dry mustard ·

Place the leg of lamb or mutton in a well-greased shallow baking dish. Sprinkle the meat with salt and red pepper. Cover the leg with sliced bacon. Add the onions and tomatoes. Bake in a 350° oven, allowing 30 minutes per pound for lamb, or 40 minutes per pound for mutton. Baste the meat in its juice frequently.

30 minutes before serving, add the cream and mustard. Serve hot, covering the meat with the sauce.

SERVES 8.

Cabrito en Salsa Marinera

Young Goat in Marine Sauce

2 pounds young goat, sliced thin · 2 tablespoons flour · 1 teaspoon salt · 1/2 teaspoon red pepper · 2 tablespoons olive oil · 3 garlic cloves, crushed · 1 medium-sized onion, chopped · 2 small bay leaves · 2 tablespoons parsley, chopped · 1 tablespoon vinegar · 1/2 cup warm water ·

I cannot promise that you can find young goat meat where you live, but it is served in many parts of Mexico, especially in the northern part of the country. Early in the morning, one can see a farmer walking to market with a young goat, still alive, draped around his neck. The Mexicans add their own flair to the preparation of goat meat, and unless you have been told what you are eating, you probably will find it delicious.

Dip the meat in a mixture of flour, salt, and red pepper. Brown on top of the stove in the oil. Add garlic, onions, bay leaves, parsley, vinegar, and water. Cover and simmer until the meat is tender, one and a half to two hours.

SERVES 4.

las aves

10

poultry

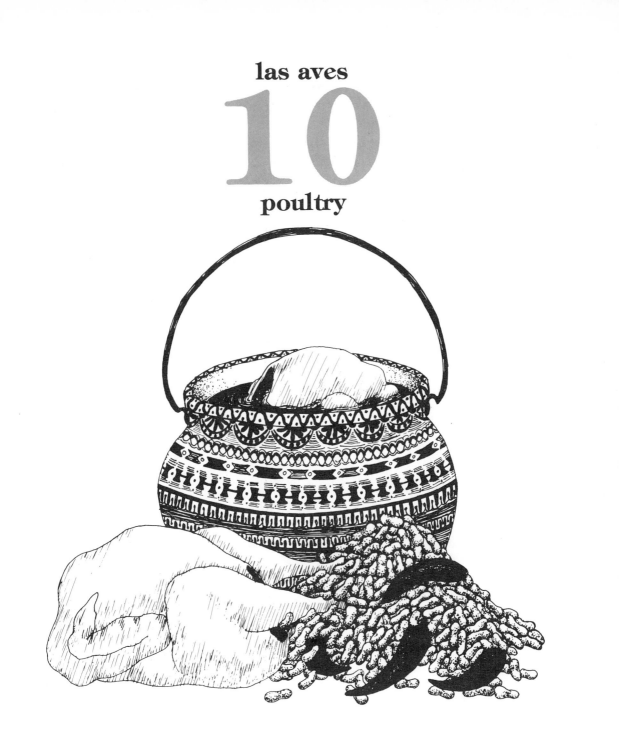

Poultry and wild fowl dishes, prepared in many exotic ways, awaited the Spanish conqueror when he arrived in Mexico. They were served to the Spaniards as a sign of friendship. Today these dishes still signify hospitality, and the Mexican cooks are skilled in the art of their preparation.

Although duck, turkey, partridge, pigeons, quail, and other fowl are served in many parts of Mexico today, the most popular dish is chicken. It may be a very simple chicken dish for the family, or an unusual cuisine for guests.

Gallina en Salsa de Aceitunas

Chicken with Olive Sauce (pictured on cover)

3 pound fricasseeing chicken, cut up · 1 small bell pepper, minced · 1 onion, minced · 1 shallot or garlic clove, minced · 1 inch stick cinnamon, or 1 teaspoon ground cinnamon · 12 green olives, sliced · 1 slice white bread, soaked in water · salt and pepper to taste · 1 teaspoon oregano · 4 cups chicken broth · 1/2 cup tomato puree · 2 tablespoons flour · 1/3 cup vegetable or olive oil · 24 whole green olives · 1/4 cup seedless raisins · 1 teaspoon vinegar ·

Simmer chicken in three quarts of salted water until tender. Chop or grind, very fine, the green pepper, onion, shallot or garlic; add cinnamon, olives, and soaked bread. Season with salt and pepper. Add to this oregano, one cup of chicken broth, and the tomato puree. Force thick mixture through strainer.

Brown flour in hot oil. Gradually stir in remaining chicken broth, which has been cooled, and finally the strained mixture. Add cooked chicken, the remaining olives, whole or sliced, and the raisins. Add vinegar. Bring to a boil; lower the fire and simmer for 30 minutes, covered. If desired, a minced hot pepper may be added to above.

SERVES 4.

Arroz con Pollo

Chicken with Rice

6 strips of bacon, cut in pieces · 1/2 large onion, chopped · 1 garlic clove, minced · 1/4 cup vegetable or olive oil · 4 pound fryer, cut up · 2 medium-sized tomatoes, peeled and chopped · 1/4 teaspoon cumin · 1 cup rice · 1-1/2 cups chicken broth · 1/2 teaspoon salt · black pepper, few grains · 1 cup cooked or canned green peas ·

Fry the bacon, but remove it from the pan before it is crisp. Sauté the onion and garlic in the bacon fat until they are soft and remove them. Add the oil to the bacon fat and brown the chicken. Remove from the pan.

Stir in the tomatoes and cumin. Add bacon, onion, garlic, chicken, and rice. Pour the chicken broth over all the ingredients; add salt and pepper.

Cover the pan and simmer at least 30 minutes or until the rice and chicken are tender. Add more broth or warm water if necessary. Add the cooked green peas before serving.

SERVES 4–5.

Pollito Tapatio

Jalisco-Style Chicken

3 pound chicken,
cut up · 1/4 cup
vinegar ·
1 tablespoon
vegetable or olive
oil · 1 chile,
chopped (any
variety of hot
pepper), or 1
tablespoon chili
powder · 5 whole
black peppercorns,
ground ·
1 medium-sized
onion, chopped ·
2 medium-sized
tomatoes, peeled
and chopped ·
2 garlic cloves,
chopped · 1 cup dry
cooking sherry ·
1 inch stick
cinnamon, or 1
teaspoon
cinnamon · 2 small
bay leaves ·
1/4 teaspoon dried
thyme ·

Simmer together in a covered pot for one and a half hours the chicken, vinegar, oil, chile, peppercorns, onion, tomatoes, garlic, sherry, and remaining spices.

Turn off the fire, allowing the chicken mixture to return to room temperature. Refrigerate overnight without uncovering the pot. Reheat before serving.

SERVES 3–4.

Pollo en Mole de Almendras

Chicken in Almond Sauce

2 pound chicken, cut up · 1/2 cup almonds, blanched · 4 chiles, or 2 medium-sized bell peppers, chopped · 2 egg yolks, mashed · 1 garlic clove, chopped · 1 teaspoon sugar · 1 teaspoon salt · 1/4 teaspoon pepper · 1/2 cup vegetable or olive oil · 2 teaspoons vinegar ·

Simmer the chicken in enough salted water to cover until tender. Save the broth that remains.

Grind or chop, very fine, the almonds; add chiles or peppers, egg yolks, and garlic. Add sugar, salt, and pepper. Brown this mixture in oil, adding the chicken broth and vinegar. Simmer 15 minutes. Add the chicken, and simmer 15 minutes more.

SERVES 4.

Pollo en Nogada

Chicken in Walnut Sauce

3 pound chicken, cut up · 2 tablespoons butter · 1/2 cup walnuts, chopped · 1/2 cup peanuts, blanched and chopped · 2 garlic cloves, minced · 1 slice white bread, diced · 2 small onions, chopped · 4 chiles, any variety red or green, or 1 medium-sized bell pepper · 3 cups chicken broth · 1 teaspoon salt · 1/4 teaspoon pepper ·

Simmer the chicken in enough salted water to cover until tender. Save the broth that remains.

Brown the walnuts, peanuts, garlic, bread, onions, and chiles in half of the butter. Dissolve this mixture in three cups of chicken broth and add the rest of the butter. Bring to a boil, lower the heat to simmer and add the chicken pieces. Season with salt and pepper. Simmer 15 minutes or until the sauce thickens.

SERVES 4.

Pollo del Jardín de San Marcos

Chicken from Saint Mark's Garden

4 pounds of chicken pieces · 1 teaspoon salt · 1 onion, chopped · 1 garlic clove, chopped · 3 medium-sized tomatoes, peeled and finely chopped · 2 cups chicken broth · 4 tablespoons vinegar · 1 inch stick cinnamon, or 1 teaspoon ground cinnamon · 1 whole clove · 3 medium-sized onions, chopped · 1/4 tablespoon oregano · 1/2 cup vegetable oil or shortening ·

Half cover the chicken pieces with salted water, onion, and garlic. Bring to a boil; then lower the heat and simmer for one hour or until the chicken is tender. Add more water if necessary.

Prepare a sauce by combining in a pan tomatoes, chicken broth, vinegar, cinnamon, clove, onions, and oregano. Bring this mixture to rapid boil; then set it aside to cool.

When the chicken is tender, drain on a paper towel. Dip the pieces in the sauce, letting them marinate about 15 minutes. Fry in hot fat until a golden brown. Serve the sauce in a side dish.

This dish may be served with fried potatoes, chorizo or link sausages, and garnishes of lettuce leaves and green chiles.

SERVES 5–6.

Pollo Exquisito

Exquisite Chicken

3 pounds chicken pieces with chicken liver · 1 large onion, thinly sliced · 1 cup dry white wine · 1/4 teaspoon nutmeg · 1 teaspoon salt · 1/4 pound butter · 1 tablespoon flour · 1 cup water or chicken broth · 1/2 teaspoon salt · 1/8 teaspoon pepper ·

Marinate the chicken pieces, except the liver, in a glass casserole dish, in onion, wine, nutmeg, and salt in the refrigerator for three or four hours. Turn the pieces occasionally to marinate all evenly.

Fry the chicken and liver in the butter. Remove the liver after 10 minutes. Mash the liver with flour, water or broth, salt, and pepper. Shake this mixture in a glass jar for smoothness. Continue to fry the chicken until it is a golden brown, about 30 minutes. Remove and drain on paper towels. Pour off all but two tablespoons of butter. Slowly add the liver mixture to the pan in which the chicken was fried, stirring with a wire whisk until the mixture has thickened. Pour over the chicken and serve hot.

SERVES 4.

Gallina en Salsa

Hen in Sauce

4–5 pound fowl, cut up · 1 teaspoon salt · 3 medium-sized onions, chopped · 3 tablespoons vegetable or olive oil · 1 tablespoon bread crumbs · 1 cup dry white wine · 1 teaspoon sugar · salt and pepper ·

Cover the chicken with water to which salt has been added. Bring to a boil; lower the fire, cover and simmer about two hours, or until tender. After cooking, refrigerate the broth that remains to use in other dishes requiring chicken broth.

For the sauce, sauté the onions in hot oil until soft. Lower the heat. Add the bread crumbs, wine, and sugar. Stir continually until the sauce thickens and is smooth. Season with salt and pepper to taste.

Pour sauce over the chicken and serve hot.

SERVES 5–6.

Pollo con Alcachofas

Chicken with Artichokes

2–3 pound frying chicken, cut up · 2 ounces (1/2 stick) butter · 1/4 cup vegetable oil · 8 artichoke leaves · 1 cup dry white wine · 1/2 cup water · 1 garlic clove, minced · juice of 1 lemon · parsley · salt and pepper ·

Sauté the pieces of chicken in the butter and oil until they are well browned. Set aside on paper towels. Cut each artichoke leaf in half and sauté in the butter and oil until very hot. Set aside on paper towels.

Pour off all but two tablespoons of shortening from the frying pan. Add wine, water, and garlic. Bring to a boil. Add chicken and artichoke leaves; lower the heat to simmer; cover the pan, and cook 30 to 45 minutes until the chicken is tender.

Place the chicken on a platter surrounded by the artichoke leaves. Sprinkle each leaf with a little salt, pepper, and a few drops of lemon juice. Garnish the chicken with parsley.

SERVES 4.

Gallina en Estofado

Stewed Hen

4–5 pound fowl ·
1/2 cup (4 ounces)
butter · 2 large
tomatoes, peeled
and chopped ·
2 garlic cloves,
minced finely ·
2 peppercorns,
ground ·
1/2 teaspoon salt ·
1 inch cinnamon
stick or
1/4 teaspoon
ground cinnamon ·
1/2 teaspoon
allspice · 2 chiles,
any variety, or
substitute 1 bell
pepper, chopped ·
1 cup dry white
wine · 1/4 cup
water · 20 green
pimiento-stuffed
olives ·

Cut, or have the butcher cut, the chicken in serving pieces. Sear the pieces in hot butter. Set aside.

In the same pot, add the tomatoes, onions, garlic, peppercorns, cinnamon, allspice, and chiles or bell pepper. Cover and cook slowly until the onions are tender. Add the wine, water, olives, and salt. Bring to a boil; add chicken; lower the heat to simmer, and cook an hour or more until the chicken is tender.

Serve on a platter with the sauce poured over the chicken.

SERVES 6.

Gallina en Mole Sabrosa

Hen in Savory Sauce

4–5 pound fowl, cut up · 1/4 cup almonds, blanched and chopped · 1 slice white bread, soaked in water and ground up to pulp · 1/4 cup seedless raisins · 5 small chiles, any variety red or green hot pepper, chopped · 1/4 cup vinegar · 1 cup orange juice · 1 teaspoon sugar · 1 teaspoon cinnamon · 3 cloves, ground · 1 teaspoon oregano · 1 teaspoon salt · 1/2 teaspoon pepper ·

Simmer chicken in enough salted water to cover. Bring to a boil; lower the fire; cover and simmer about two hours or until nearly tender. Cooking time will vary somewhat, depending on the age of the fowl. A 4–5 pound fowl will be from 5 to 9 months old and will take longer to cook to tenderness.

Make a sauce by blending together in a large pot the almonds, bread, raisins, chiles, vinegar, orange juice, sugar, cinnamon, cloves, oregano, salt, and pepper. Place the pieces of chicken in the sauce. Bring to a boil. Lower the heat and simmer for 30 minutes, or until the chicken is tender.

Serve the chicken covered with the sauce.

SERVES 6.

170

Gallina en Salsa de Almendras

Hen in Almond Sauce

4–5 pound fowl, cut up · 1 teaspoon salt · 2 ounces butter · 1/4 cup vegetable or olive oil · 3 large tomatoes, peeled and chopped · 2 medium-sized onions, chopped · 1 slice bread, cut in half inch cubes · 1 cup almonds, blanched and chopped · 1 green chile pepper, or 1/4 cup bell pepper, chopped · 1/4 cup raisins · 1 cup chicken broth ·

Simmer the chicken in enough salted water to cover until nearly tender, about two hours.

Fry the tomatoes, onions, and bread in the butter and oil until the onions are soft and the bread is a golden brown. Add almonds, chopped peppers, raisins, chicken, and one cup of the liquid in which the chicken was cooking. Cover and simmer for 30 minutes, or until the sauce thickens.

SERVES 6.

Gallina en Pebre

Hen in Pepper Sauce

4-1/2–5 pound roasting chicken · 1 teaspoon salt · 1 tablespoon shortening · 2 large tomatoes, peeled and chopped · 1 large onion, chopped · 3 garlic cloves, chopped · 1 small green hot chile, or 1 tablespoon chili powder · 1/4 cup seedless raisins · 2 hard-boiled eggs, peeled and chopped · 1 cup cooked ham, diced · 12 pimiento-filled green olives · 1/4 cup almonds, blanched and chopped · 1 small bay leaf · 1/2 teaspoon allspice · 1 cup cooking sherry · salt and pepper to taste ·

Simmer the whole chicken in enough salted water to cover until tender, about two to two and a half hours. Save the liquid in which the chicken was cooked. Remove skin and bones from the chicken.

Fry tomatoes, onion, garlic, and chiles in shortening for 10 minutes. Add raisins, eggs, ham, olives, almonds, bay leaf, allspice, sherry, chicken, and a half a cup of the broth in which the chicken was cooked. Salt and pepper to taste. Simmer for 30 minutes or more to allow the seasonings to blend together.

SERVES 6–8.

Timbal de Pollo

Kettledrums of Chicken

4-pound chicken ·
1 teaspoon salt ·
1 medium-sized
onion, chopped ·
4 garlic cloves,
chopped ·
2 tablespoons
butter · 1 large
tomato, peeled and
chopped · 1 small
bay leaf · salt and
pepper ·
2 tablespoons
flour · 1/2 cup
water or chicken
broth · 12-ounce
package
pre-prepared
biscuits (10
biscuits) ·

Simmer the whole chicken in enough salted water to cover until tender, about two hours. Remove skin and bones from the chicken. Chop the meat in small pieces.

Brown the onion and garlic in butter. Add tomato, cooked chicken, bay leaf, and salt and pepper to taste. Mix the flour and water or broth together. Shake them together in a glass jar for a smoother mixture. Stir this into the chicken mixture and continue to stir until the mixture is thick, about 10 minutes. Remove bay leaf.

For the kettledrums, roll the biscuit dough until it is about 1/4 inch thick. Place five of the biscuits on an ungreased baking sheet. Place an even amount of the chicken mixture on each of the flat biscuits. Top each with another flat biscuit. Bake in a 475° oven for 10 minutes. Serve hot.

SERVES 5.

Budín Azteca

Aztec Pudding (Chicken)

1/2 medium-sized onion, chopped · 1 tablespoon vegetable oil · 3 medium-sized tomatoes, peeled and chopped · 1/2 teaspoon salt · 4 eggs, separated · 12 corn tortillas, frozen or home-made · 4 green chiles (canned), chopped · 2 chicken breasts, cooked and shredded · 3/4 cup Romano cheese, grated ·

Sauté the onion in oil until soft. Add tomatoes and salt; simmer. Beat the egg whites to a peak; beat the egg yolks and blend into the whites.

Heat each tortilla in an ungreased heavy frying pan over medium heat until warm but not crisp. Dip each tortilla in the egg mixture. Place flat in ovenproof shallow dishes or baking sheets. The edges of the tortillas should turn up. On each tortilla, place chiles, chicken, tomato and onion mixture, cheese, and top with the rest of the beaten eggs. Bake in a 350° oven for 15 minutes or until the eggs are thoroughly cooked.

SERVES 4–6.

Flautas de Pollo

Chicken Flutes

12 corn tortillas, frozen or home-made · 2 cups cooked chicken, shredded · 1 teaspoon salt · 2/3 cup shortening · 2 cups green sauce · 1/2 cup sharp cheddar cheese, grated ·

Heat each tortilla in an ungreased heavy frying pan over medium heat until warm but not crisp. Salt the chicken and place a heaping tablespoon on each tortilla. Use all of the mixture. Roll the tortillas as tightly as possible, holding them together with toothpicks. Fry in shortening until golden brown. Drain on paper towels.

Serve with green sauce (see page 66 "Green Tomato Sauce"), or use commercial green sauce. Garnish with cheese.

SERVES 4–6.

Croquetas de Pollo

Chicken Croquettes

2 tablespoons butter · 1 small onion, finely chopped · 3 tablespoons flour · 1 cup chicken broth · 1/2 teaspoon salt · 1/4 teaspoon pepper · 2 cups cooked chicken, ground or chopped finely · 1 egg, beaten · bread crumbs · vegetable oil for deep fat frying ·

Heat butter in frying pan; lightly brown onion. Blend in the flour; and slowly add broth, stirring continually over low heat until the mixture is smooth and thick. Season with salt and pepper. Add chicken, and refrigerate to cool thoroughly.

Shape into croquettes. Dip in egg, and then in the bread crumbs. Fry in deep fat at 380° for about five minutes or until the croquettes are a golden brown.

SERVES 6.

Pavo Relleno

Stuffed Turkey

18–20 pound turkey · salt and pepper · juice of 1 lemon · 1/4 pound bacon, sliced · 1/4 cup shortening · 1 large onion, chopped · 1/2 pound lean pork loin, cut in strips · 1/2 cup tomato paste · 1/2 cup pimiento-stuffed olives · 1/4 cup vinegar · 2 large tomatoes, peeled and chopped · 1/4 cup almonds, blanched and chopped · 6 jalapeño peppers, chopped · 1 ripe banana, mashed · 1 apple, peeled and sliced · 1 carrot, scraped and diced · 2 tablespoons sugar · 1/4 teaspoon cinnamon · 1/2 teaspoon salt · 1/4 cup olive oil · 1 cup dry white wine ·

Sprinkle the turkey with salt, pepper, and lemon juice inside and out before stuffing.

Brown the bacon; drain on paper towel, and slice or crumble in small pieces. Add shortening to the bacon grease; simmer over a medium fire onion, pork, tomato paste, olives, vinegar, tomatoes, almonds, Jalapeño peppers, banana, apple, carrot, sugar, cinnamon, salt, and the cooked bacon. Simmer about 10 minutes, and stuff the neck of the turkey and fasten with a skewer. Next fill the cavity and fasten the opening with aluminum pins.

Place the stuffed turkey breast side up in a large roasting pan. Brush the fowl with oil. Add wine to the pan and bake in a 350° oven, allowing 15 minutes per pound cooking time. Baste frequently with the wine and the turkey drippings.

ALLOW 3/4 TO 1 POUND OF TURKEY PER SERVING.

Pavo Relleno con Castanas

Turkey Stuffed with Chestnuts

12–16 pound turkey ·
1-1/2 pounds chestnuts ·
1 teaspoon vegetable oil ·
1/2 pound pork ·
salt and pepper ·
1/4 cup olive oil ·
1/2 cup chicken broth ·

Shell the chestnuts by slitting the skin with two crossing gashes on the flat side of the nut with a sharp knife. Place in a heavy skillet in oil over low heat. Cover and shake until the skins loosen and the shells and skin can be removed. The chestnuts may also be placed in boiling water for 15 to 20 minutes. Drain and remove the shells and skin. Shell and mash or chop coarsely.

Brown the pork in oil and season with salt and pepper. Cut the pork in small pieces (about 1/4 inch square) and mix with the chestnuts.

Stuff neck of the turkey with chestnut and pork mixture, and fasten with a skewer. Next fill the cavity and fasten the opening with aluminum pins.

Place the stuffed bird breast side up in a large roasting pan. Brush the fowl with oil. Add chicken broth to the pan for basting. Bake in a 350° oven, allowing 12 minutes per pound cooking time. Baste frequently with the turkey drippings.

ALLOW 3/4 TO 1 POUND OF TURKEY PER SERVING.

Pato Asado

Roast Duck

4 pound duck ·
juice of 1 lemon ·
1/4 cup vinegar ·
3 medium-sized
onions, chopped ·
2 cups water ·
1/4 cup olive oil ·
3 large tomatoes,
peeled and
chopped · 3 garlic
cloves, chopped ·
1/2 teaspoon salt ·
1/4 teaspoon
pepper ·
18 pimiento-stuffed
green olives ·
12 hot chiles ·

Clean the duck, and singe if necessary. Rub the duck with lemon juice. Cut into six portions. Add vinegar, onions, and water; simmer covered for one hour.

Fry tomatoes, garlic, salt, and pepper for five minutes. Cover the duck with this sauce and simmer, uncovered, until the duck is brown and tender, about 30 minutes.

Serve covered with the sauce and garnished with olives and chiles.

SERVES 6.

Pato Guisado

Stewed Duck

4–5 pound duck ·
1/2 teaspoon salt ·
1/4 cup
shortening ·
1 medium-sized
onion, chopped ·
1/2 cup cooked
ham, diced ·
2 slices bacon,
shredded ·
1/4 teaspoon
pepper ·
1/2 teaspoon salt ·
1/2 cup water ·
1 tablespoon bread
crumbs · 1 sprig
parsley, finely
chopped ·

Rinse the duck under cold water, and singe if necessary. Cut into six serving pieces. Sprinkle the pieces with salt. Fry in shortening over low heat for 30 minutes. Turn the duck to brown on all sides.

Add onion, ham, bacon, pepper, and the additional salt. Cover and simmer 15 minutes. Then add water, bread crumbs, and parsley and simmer uncovered for 15 minutes.

SERVES 6.

Pato en Jugo de Naranja

Duck in Orange Juice

4–5 pound duck ·
2 garlic cloves ·
2 medium-sized
onions, chopped ·
3 medium-sized
tomatoes, peeled
and chopped ·
2 sprigs parsley,
chopped · 1/4 cup
seedless raisins ·
1/4 cup almonds,
blanched and
chopped · 1/2 cup
vinegar · 3 cups
orange juice · 1
teaspoon salt ·

Rinse the duck under cold water, and singe if necessary. Cut into six serving pieces. Place in a pot with garlic, onion, tomatoes, parsley, raisins, almonds, vinegar, orange juice, and salt.

Cover the pot and cook over low heat for three hours. Stir from time to time to prevent sticking. Serve hot in the sauce.

SERVES 6.

Pichones Rellenos

Stuffed Pigeons

4 small pigeons or
Rock Cornish hens ·
1 veal cutlet ·
1 small onion,
chopped · 2 slices
bacon ·
1 hard-boiled egg,
peeled and
chopped · salt ·
pepper · butter ·
1 cup chicken broth
or water ·

Rinse the fowl under cold water, and singe if necessary. Brown the veal with the onion and bacon. Cut the veal and bacon in small pieces. Add the egg to the veal mixture and stuff the fowls. Place breast side up in a shallow baking dish. Brush generously with soft butter. Sprinkle with salt and pepper. Add chicken stock or water. Bake in a 350° oven for one hour or until tender. Add more stock or water if necessary.

SERVES 4.

Pichones con Chicharos

Pigeons with Peas

4 small pigeons,
squabs, or Rock
Cornish hens ·
4 slices bacon, cut
up · 1/4 cup
vegetable oil ·
4 small onions,
chopped · 1 cup
warm water ·
2 sprigs parsley,
finely chopped ·
1/2 teaspoon salt ·
1/4 teaspoon
pepper · 1 can (17
ounces) sweet
green peas,
drained ·

Rinse the fowl under cold water, and singe if necessary. Sauté in bacon and vegetable oil, browning on all sides. Brown onions. Add water, parsley, salt, and pepper. Cover and simmer for one hour. Add peas and simmer for 30 more minutes.

SERVES 4.

Perdices a la Vinagreta

Vinegar Sauce Partridges

4 small partridges
or Rock Cornish
hens ·
1 medium-sized
onion,
chopped · 1/4 cup
vegetable or olive
oil · 1 cup vinegar ·
2 garlic cloves,
minced · 1 small
bay leaf · 2 sprigs
parsley, finely
chopped ·
1/4 teaspoon thyme
· 1/4 cup water ·

Rinse the fowl under cold water, and singe if necessary. Brown the fowl and onion in the oil. Add vinegar, garlic, bay leaf, parsley, thyme, and water. Cover and simmer for one hour or until the birds are tender. Serve with rice (see page 62, "Tropical Rice").

SERVES 4.

Perdices en Salsita

Partridges in a Little Sauce

4 small partridges
or Rock Cornish
hens · 1 teaspoon
salt · 1/2 cup flour ·
2 tablespoons
butter · 1/4 cup
vegetable or olive
oil · 1/4 cup
almonds,
blanched · 1 clove
garlic, minced ·
2 sprigs parsley,
finely chopped ·
1 square
unsweetened
chocolate ·
1 tablespoon
vinegar ·
1 tablespoon olive
oil · 1 cup chicken
broth or water ·
1 small bay leaf ·

Clean, quarter, and salt the fowls. Shake the birds in a paper sack with the flour. Fry in a moderately hot skillet in butter and oil until brown. Drain on paper towels.

Meanwhile, prepare the sauce by combining the almonds, garlic, parsley, chocolate, vinegar, oil, broth, and bay leaf in a large pot. Add the fowls. Cover and simmer for one hour or until the birds are tender. Add more liquid if necessary.

SERVES 4.

Codornices a la mejicana

Mexican-Style Quail

4 quails, partridges, or Rock Cornish hens · 2 medium onions, diced · 1/2 cup dry white wine · 1/2 teaspoon salt · 1/4 teaspoon pepper · 1/3 cup almonds, blanched and chopped · 1/2 cup cooked ham, diced · 2 hard-boiled egg yolks, mashed · 3 large tomatoes, peeled and chopped · 2 tablespoons butter · 1/2 cup cooking sherry ·

Simmer the fowl with the onions, wine, salt, and pepper for one hour. Add water if the mixture cooks too dry. Save the broth that remains.

Meanwhile, cook the almonds, ham, egg yolks, and tomatoes in butter until the tomatoes are soft, about 15 minutes. Add the fowl and the broth to the tomato mixture. Simmer 15 minutes. Add sherry and cook 15 more minutes.

SERVES 4.

Tortolas a la mejicana

Mexican-Style Turtledoves

10 turtledoves or 5
Rock Cornish hens ·
1 teaspoon salt ·
4 tablespoons
butter · 1/2 cup
cooked ham,
diced ·
2 tablespoons
flour · 1 cup dry
white wine · 1 cup
chicken broth ·
3 small onions,
chopped · 2 garlic
cloves, chopped ·
1 small bay leaf ·
1/4 teaspoon
pepper ·

Clean the birds in cold water; sprinkle with salt; and fry in butter until golden brown. Add the ham; sprinkle the fowl and ham with flour. Add wine, broth, onions, garlic, bay leaf, and pepper. Cover and simmer one hour or until the birds are tender. Serve fowl on a platter; cover them with the sauce.

SERVES 5.

los huevos
11
egg dishes

In Mexico, one does not run down to the super-market, or "supermercado," as it is called in that country, to buy a dozen eggs. Eggs have always been considered a delicacy. They are sold individually and used primarily for garnishes or sauces. Frequently, a single egg may be placed before the altar in the village church or the city cathedral as a tribute made by an impoverished worshiper as his most prized possession. Egg dishes, in this chapter prepared with the Mexican gusto, are served among the wealthier class.

Huevos Rancheros

Ranch Eggs

1 onion, chopped · 1 garlic clove, chopped · 1 tablespoon butter · 1 cup tomato purée · 1 mountain chile pepper, or any variety of small green hot peppers · 6 tortillas · shortening for deep fat frying · 6 eggs · 2 avocados, peeled and sliced · 1 teaspoon salt · 1/4 teaspoon pepper ·

Brown the onion and garlic in the butter. Add purée and chile pepper, and season with salt and pepper. Stir for about 15 minutes until the mixture is thick. Set aside to cool.

Deep fat fry each tortilla until a light brown. Fry the eggs in a separate frying pan to which a little shortening has been added. Place a tortilla on each plate; put a fried egg on the tortilla; and cover the egg with the sauce. Garnish each plate with slices of avocado, if you wish.

SERVES 6.

Huevos Rancheros

Ranch-Style Eggs

1 cup onions chopped · 1 garlic clove, chopped · 3 tablespoons butter · 3 cups tomatoes, peeled and chopped · 2 tablespoons jalapeño sauce · 1/2 cup sharp cheddar cheese, grated · 1 teaspoon salt · 1/2 teaspoon pepper · 8 tortillas · oil for frying · 8 eggs, fried ·

Here is a slightly different version of the preceding "Huevos Rancheros" recipe.

Sauté the onions and garlic in butter. Add tomatoes, jalapeño sauce (a canned or bottled commercial sauce available at your local grocery store), and cheese, and season with salt and pepper. Bring to a boil; lower the heat and simmer, uncovered, for 15 minutes. Stir from time to time. Serve the sauce either hot or cold.

Deep fat fry each tortilla until light brown. Dip in the sauce and place on a plate. Top each tortilla with a fried egg, and cover the egg with the sauce.

SERVES 8.

Longaniza con Huevo

Pork Sausage with Egg

2 tablespoons vegetable or olive oil · 1 small onion, chopped · 4 canned green chiles, chopped · 2 tomatoes, peeled and chopped · 1 pound ground pork sausage · 1/4 cup water · 4 eggs, slightly beaten · 1 teaspoon salt ·

Melt the oil in a heavy skillet over low heat; sauté onions and chiles about four minutes or until onion is soft. Add tomatoes, sausage, and water. Stir from time to time with a spoon. Simmer about 20 minutes until the sausage is well done.

Stir in the beaten eggs, and continue to stir with a spoon until the eggs are firm. Serve immediately.

SERVES 4.

Huevos Revueltos a la mejicana

Scrambled Eggs Mexican Style

2 tablespoons butter · 8 eggs, well-beaten · 2 tablespoons light cream or milk · 2 small tomatoes, peeled and chopped · 1/2 teaspoon pepper · 3 tablespoons canned green chiles, chopped · 2 tablespoons onions, chopped · 2 tablespoons parsley, chopped · 1/2 cup mild cheddar cheese, grated · 1-1/2 teaspoons salt ·

Melt butter in heavy frying pan. Beat the eggs thoroughly with the cream; pour into the pan. Allow the eggs to set a moment; then add tomatoes, green chiles, onions, parsley, cheese, and season with salt and pepper. Stir continually with a spatula or spoon over medium heat until the eggs are dry. Serve immediately.

SERVES 5–6.

Huevos Revueltos

Scrambled Eggs

1 small onion,
chopped · 1 garlic
clove, chopped ·
1 green chile
pepper, chopped ·
2 tablespoons
bacon fat or
vegetable oil ·
1/2 cup tomato
purée · 1 teaspoon
salt · 1/2 teaspoon
pepper · 6 eggs,
beaten ·

Sauté the onion, garlic, and chile peppers in the fat until the onion is soft and light brown. Add tomato purée; season with salt and pepper. Stir in the beaten eggs with a spoon and continue to stir, scraping the sides and bottom of the pan, until the eggs are firm. Serve immediately.

SERVES 4.

Huevos en Camisas

Eggs in Jackets

6 eggs, separated ·
butter · 1 teaspoon
salt · 1 sprig
parsley, chopped ·

Grease muffin tins generously with butter. Separate the egg yolks from the whites. Place each egg yolk carefully in a muffin tin. Beat the egg whites until stiff but not dry, and blend in salt and parsley. Cover each yolk with the beaten egg whites. Bake in a 350° oven about 15 minutes, or until the egg whites are lightly browned. Serve immediately.

SERVES 6.

Huevos en Cazoleta

Eggs in Pan

6 slices boiled ham · 6 eggs · 1-8 ounce can tomato sauce · 6 white bread slices, toasted ·

Line muffin tins with one slice of boiled ham. Carefully break an egg over each slice of ham. Spoon one tablespoon of tomato sauce over each egg. Sprinkle with salt.

Bake in a 350° oven about 15 minutes, or until the eggs are firm. Carefully lift the ham and egg from the muffin tin and serve on a slice of toast.

SERVES 6.

Huevos Exquisitos

Exquisite Eggs

1 onion, chopped fine · 1 tablespoon shortening · 2 chile peppers, any variety red or green small hot pepper · 1 cup tomato purée · 1/4 cup water · 6 tortillas · vegetable oil for deep fat frying · 15-1/2 ounce can refried beans · 6 eggs · 1/4 cup longhorn cheese, grated · salt and pepper to taste ·

Prepare a sauce by lightly browning the onion in the shortening. Add chile peppers, tomato purée, and water. Simmer for 10 minutes, stirring occasionally, and set aside. The mixture should be thick.

Deep fat fry each tortilla until a light brown. Drain on paper towels. Separately, fry the eggs. On each plate, place a tortilla covered with refried beans; and top each with a hot fried egg sprinkled with cheese. Salt and pepper to taste.

Serve the remaining tomato sauce in a side dish.

SERVES 6.

Huevos en Salsa Verde

Eggs in Green Sauce

6 eggs, hard-boiled · 1 medium-sized onion, chopped · 2 sprigs parsley, chopped · 1 tablespoon olive oil · 1 tablespoon vinegar · 1/4 cup green salad olives, chopped · 1/2 teaspoon salt · 1/4 teaspoon pepper ·

Hard boil the eggs; remove the shell; and cut each egg into four sections lengthwise.

Prepare a sauce by mixing the onions, parsley, oil, vinegar, olives, salt, and pepper.

Place the eggs on a platter and top them with the sauce. Refrigerate one hour before serving.

SERVES 6.

Huevos con Camarones

Eggs with Shrimp

8 eggs, hard-boiled · 1 teaspoon salt · 1/2 cup mayonnaise, commercial or home made · 1-3/4 ounce can peeled shrimp ·

Serve these as an appetizer, or as a dish with a cold supper. I have done both, and they are always a winner.

Hard boil the eggs; remove shells and cut in half lengthwise. Remove the yolks; add salt and mayonnaise to the yolk; mix thoroughly with a fork. Add more mayonnaise, if necessary.

Fill the whites with the yolk mixture. On each, place one or two small shrimp. Top each shrimp with mayonnaise and chill in the refrigerator for at least an hour before serving.

MAKES 16; SERVES 8.

Preparation of Omelets

If the eggs have been refrigerated, allow them to reach room temperature. Then beat eggs with the milk; add the seasoning. Heat butter or other shortening in a frying pan over medium heat. Lower the heat, and add the beaten eggs. Cover the pan, but periodically lift the egg mixture carefully with a spatula as it cooks on the bottom, tipping the pan so that the uncooked mixture on the top will run to the bottom. When the bottom is brown and the egg mixture firm, fold the omelet in half in the shape of a semicircle and serve hot.

Huevos a la mejicana

Mexican-Style Eggs

3 eggs, beaten ·
2 tablespoons
milk · 1 small
onion, chopped ·
1 teaspoon parsley,
chopped · 1/4
teaspoon salt · a
few grains of
pepper ·
1 tablespoon
vegetable oil ·

Beat the eggs with the milk; add onion and parsley. Season with salt and pepper. Empty into a greased frying pan or greased omelet pan over a low fire. Cover the pan, but be careful not to burn the omelet. Cook until the bottom is brown and the egg mixture firm. (Refer to "Preparation of Omelets.") Fold the omelet in half in the shape of a semicircle.

SERVES 2.

Tortilla de Champiñones

Mushroom Omelet

2 cups mushrooms · 2 tablespoons parsley, chopped · 1 garlic clove, chopped · 1 tablespoon olive oil, or vegetable oil · 4 eggs, beaten · 1 tablespoon milk · 1/4 teaspoon salt · a few grains of pepper ·

Wash and slice the mushrooms. Sauté mushrooms, parsley, and garlic in oil for five minutes.

Beat the eggs with the milk, salt, and pepper. Add the eggs to the mushroom mixture, and follow the directions for "Preparation of Omelets."

SERVES 3–4.

Tortilla de Camerones

Shrimp Omelet

1 cup cooked shrimp · 4 eggs · 2 tablespoons heavy cream · 1/4 teaspoon salt · a few grains of pepper ·

Unless the shrimp are quite small, slice them in half.

Beat the eggs, cream, salt, and pepper together, and follow the instructions for "Preparation of Omelets." Just before folding the omlet, add the shrimp. Fold and serve hot.

SERVES 2.

Tortilla de Cebolla y Papa

Onion and Potato Omelet

2 large white
potatoes, peeled
and chopped ·
1 onion, chopped ·
2 tablespoons
vegetable or olive
oil · 1/2 teaspoon
salt · 4 eggs,
beaten ·
12 pimiento-stuffed
olives ·

Fry the potatoes and onions in oil about five minutes until the potatoes begin to brown but are not dark. Add salt, and mash with a fork. Fold the potato and onion mixture into the beaten eggs. Follow the directions for "Preparation of Omelets." Garnish with olives.

For a light supper, serve with a green salad.

SERVES 3–4.

Tortilla de Queso

Cheese Omelet

6 eggs ·
4 tablespoons
milk · 1/2 teaspoon
salt · a few grains
of pepper ·
3 tablespoons
butter or bacon
drippings · 1/2 cup
sharp cheddar
cheese, grated ·

Beat the eggs with milk, salt, and pepper. Follow the directions for "Preparation of Omelets." Just before folding the omelet, add the cheese.

SERVES 4–5.

los legumbres

vegetables

In the beginning was corn; thus it was before the discovery of America and continues to be today. Not a day goes by without the Mexican eating corn in one form or another. Corn tortillas are a part of every meal. Hot and steaming corn on the cob is sold from portable carts on street corners in any part of Mexico. Basically, corn dishes are prepared the same way today as they were hundreds of years ago by the Indian women.

In addition to corn, the discovery of America introduced beans, tomatoes, pepper, potatoes, and a number of other root vegetables to the diets of the Europeans.

As Mexicans are not very fond of potatoes or plain boiled vegetables, they tend to disguise them in a number of ways.

Frijoles Refritos

Refried Beans

1 pound dry pinto beans · 7 cups water · 2 garlic cloves, minced · 1/4 teaspoon cumin · 3 tablespoons of bacon fat · 1 teaspoon salt · 1/2 large onion, minced · 1/2 cup shredded cheddar cheese ·

Wash the beans and put them in a large pot. Add the water, cumin, and garlic; cook over a low fire for about 1-1/2 hours. Then add the bacon fat, salt, and onion and cook about 1-1/2 hours more or until beans are soft.

Be sure there is plenty of water in the pot at all times and stir the beans occasionally.

The beans may be served as they come from the pot, or they may be mashed or put in a blender and topped with shredded cheese before serving.

MAKES 6 CUPS.

Papas duquesa

Duchess Potatoes

6 medium-sized potatoes, peeled and quartered · 4 cups water · 1/2 teaspoon salt · a few grains of pepper · a few grains of nutmeg · 3 egg yolks, well beaten · 1 egg white, well beaten · butter ·

Cook the potatoes in salted water about 20 minutes, or until they are soft. Drain, and place on the heat a few more minutes to dry the potatoes; then mash. Add pepper, nutmeg; blend in egg yolks and egg white.

Place in individual servings in a greased baking dish. Mash down a little depression in the middle of each serving and place in it a dot of butter.

Brown in a 400° oven and serve hot.

SERVES 4–5.

Papas con Salsa Verde

Potatoes with Green Sauce

2 onions, chopped · 3 garlic cloves, chopped · 2 tablespoons vegetable or olive oil · 6 medium-sized potatoes, peeled and sliced · 2 tablespoons flour · 3 sprigs parsley, chopped · 2 egg yolks, beaten · 1/2 teaspoon salt · juice of 1/2 lemon ·

Sauté the onion and garlic in oil until the onions are soft but not brown. Add the potatoes and enough warm water to cover. Add flour and parsley to give the sauce a green tint.

Cover and simmer until the potatoes are tender. Add egg yolks, salt, and lemon juice. Simmer 10 more minutes. Serve immediately.

SERVES 4–6.

Papas con Chicharos

Potatoes with Peas

2 cups green peas, shelled · 4 small whole onions · 4 large potatoes, peeled and quartered · 1 teaspoon salt · 4 chile peppers, any variety, chopped · 2 medium tomatoes, peeled and chopped · 2 tablespoons olive oil · 1/4 teaspoon thyme · 1/4 teaspoon leaf oregano · 2 tablespoons vinegar ·

Cook the peas, onions, and potatoes in salted water to cover until all are tender, about 20 minutes.

Meanwhile, fry the chiles and tomatoes in the oil for five minutes. Add thyme, oregano, vinegar and salt to taste. Add this mixture to the pan in which the peas, onions, and potatoes are cooking. Boil until 3/4 of the liquid is absorbed.

SERVES 6.

Chicaros con Crema

Peas with Cream

1/4 cup butter · 1 tablespoon flour · 2 cups water · 2 cups green peas, shelled · 1 sprig parsley, chopped · 1 small onion, whole · 1 teaspoon salt · 1 cup thick cream · 1 tablespoon sugar ·

Melt the butter in a saucepan; blend in the flour. Slowly add the water, stirring continually for five minutes. Add peas, parsley, onion, and salt. Cook over a very low fire for 20 minutes or until the peas are tender.

Remove onion and drain peas. Add the cream and sugar to the peas, and continue to cook a few minutes more until the cream is warm.

SERVES 5–6.

Garbanzos con Tocino

Chickpeas with Bacon

2 cups dried chickpeas · 1/2 pound smoked bacon, diced · 2 small onions, sliced · 1 small bay leaf · 1/4 teaspoon thyme · 1 teaspoon salt · 2 tablespoons olive oil · 1 tablespoon tomato paste · 2 cups broth · 1 carrot, scraped and sliced · 1/4 pound ground sausage ·

Soak the chickpeas for 24 hours in water to cover. Drain; add fresh water to cover; bring to a boil; lower the heat to simmer; add bacon and cook two hours. Add onions, bay leaf, thyme, salt, and one tablespoon of olive oil; cook for 45 minutes more.

Drain the peas, and reserve the broth. In the same pot, heat the remaining tablespoon of olive oil, the tomato paste, two cups of the reserved broth, the carrot, sausage, and finally the bacon and peas.

Cover the pot and simmer 30 more minutes.

MAKES 5–6 CUPS.

Espinacas con Garbanzos

Spinach with Chickpeas

2-1/2 cups dried chickpeas · 2 teaspoons salt · 1 small hot red pepper · 2 pounds spinach · 1 tablespoon olive oil · 4 garlic cloves, chopped · 1 tablespoon bread crumbs · 2 tablespoons vinegar ·

Soak the chickpeas for 24 hours in water to cover. Drain; add fresh water to cover, 1 tablespoon of salt, and the red pepper. Simmer for two to two and a half hours.

Wash the spinach under running water. Place in another pan to which one teaspoon of salt has been added and cook over low heat. There should be enough water on the spinach leaves without adding additional water. Cook 10 minutes, covered.

In a frying pan, melt the oil and brown the garlic and bread crumbs. Add this mixture and the vinegar to the spinach.

Drain the chickpeas and place in a large serving bowl. Cover the peas with the spinach.

SERVES 12.

Ejotes a la castellana

Castillian-Style Green Beans

2 pounds green beans · 1 cup water · 1 teaspoon salt · 2 garlic cloves, chopped · 2 sprigs parsley, chopped · 2 whole hot red peppers, chopped · 1 tablespoon olive oil ·

Wash beans; remove ends and strings if necessary. Snap in two, or if the beans are small, leave whole. Cover and boil rapidly in one cup of salted water for 20 minutes or until beans are tender.

Simmer the garlic, parsley, and red peppers in the olive oil until the garlic begins to brown. Add to the beans and mix well. Season with more salt if necessary. Place on a platter and serve hot.

SERVES 8.

Ejotes en Salsa

Green Beans in Sauce

1 pound green beans · 1/2 cup water · 1/2 teaspoon salt · 3 tablespoons butter · 2 tablespoons flour · 1 cup milk · 1 egg yolk, beaten · 1/2 teaspoon lemon juice · red pepper, few grains · 1/2 teaspoon salt · 1/4 teaspoon pepper ·

Wash beans; remove ends and strings if necessary. Snap in two, or if the beans are small, leave whole. Cover and boil rapidly in salted water for 20 minutes.

Prepare a sauce by melting a tablespoon of the butter in a frying pan; blend in the flour, and gradually add the milk, stirring continually over a low fire for five minutes. Remove from the heat and blend in the egg yolk. Return to the heat and add the remaining 2 tablespoons of butter, lemon juice, and red pepper; season with salt and pepper. Simmer five minutes.

Drain the green beans; cover with the sauce and serve hot.

SERVES 4.

Esparragos con Mayonesa

Asparagus with Mayonnaise

1 pound asparagus · 1 teaspoon salt · mayonnaise, commercial or homemade · parsley for garnish ·

Keep asparagus refrigerated until ready to use, and use as soon as possible, as asparagus does not keep well.

Asparagus should be cooked in a deep pan with a lid. Place asparagus in the pan with the tender tips at the top. Fill the pan with about two inches of water, add salt, cover, and boil about 16 minutes. Check the lower stalks for tenderness.

Serve with commercial mayonnaise or use the recipe for mayonnaise on page 70. Garnish the platter with parsley.

SERVES 4.

201

Esparragos a la romana

Roman-Style Asparagus

1 pound asparagus · 1 teaspoon salt · 6 tablespoons butter · 3 tablespoons lemon juice · 3 egg yolks, beaten · 1 tablespoon heavy cream · a pinch of nutmeg · 1 tablespoon parmesan cheese, grated · 1/4 teaspoon salt · cayenne pepper, few grains ·

Follow the preceding recipe for cooking the asparagus, or if you prefer, cook the stalks and tips separately. Cut the stalks off about two inches from the end. Place them in enough boiling water to cover, to which salt has been added. Cover the pan and boil twenty minutes. The tips should be cooked standing upright, tied in a bunch, on a rack with just enough boiling water to cover the rack. Cover and steam cook 15 minutes.

In a double boiler, melt the butter and gradually add the lemon juice, egg yolks, cream, nutmeg, cheese, salt, and pepper. Cook over very low heat, stirring continually for three or four minutes until the mixture thickens.

Drain the asparagus; cover with the sauce and serve immediately.

SERVES 4.

Jitomates Rellenos con Queso y Jamón

Tomatoes Stuffed with Cheese and Ham

6 red tomatoes ·
salt · 1/2 cup
cooked ham,
chopped · 1/2 cup
sharp Cheddar
cheese, grated ·
3 tablespoons
melted butter ·
1 egg, beaten ·
1 teaspoon parsley,
chopped ·
shortening ·
parsley, large
leaves for garnish ·

Select firm tomatoes of uniform size and shape. Wash and cut about a 1-1/2 inch circle from the stem end. Remove seeds and pulp with a teaspoon or with a scoop for making melon balls. Sprinkle the cavity with salt. Mix the tomato pulp with ham, half of the cheese, butter, egg, and parsley. Stuff each tomato with this mixture. Top with the remaining cheese.

Place the tomatoes in a shallow baking dish which has been lightly coated with shortening. Bake at 375° for 30 minutes. Place on a round platter with garnishes of parsley between each tomato.

SERVES 6.

Habas a la asturiana

Asturian-Style Lima Beans

3 pounds lima
beans · 1 onion,
chopped · 1 garlic
clove ·
3 tablespoons olive
oil · 1/2 cup
cooked ham,
diced · 4 carrots,
scraped and
sliced · 6 new
potatoes, peeled ·
1 cup dry white
wine ·
1/2 teaspoon salt ·
1/4 teaspoon red
pepper ·

Shell the beans. Place in a large pan.

Sauté the onion and garlic in the olive oil until the onion is soft. Add the onion and garlic to the pan with the beans; then add ham, carrots, potatoes, wine, salt, and red pepper. Cover and boil rapidly for 30 minutes or until the potatoes and carrots are tender. Add water to the pan, if necessary. Drain and serve hot.

SERVES 4–5.

Zanahorias con Jamón

Carrots with Ham

1 pound carrots ·
1/2 teaspoon salt ·
1 cup water ·
2 tablespoons olive
oil · 2 tablespoons
flour · 2 cups broth
or warm water ·
1 cup cooked ham,
chopped · salt and
pepper to taste ·

Cut the top end and a half inch of the bottom end from the carrots. Scrape and cut in half lengthwise. Small young carrots may be cooked whole. Place in rapidly boiling salted water. Cover and cook about 15 minutes until the carrots are tender. Cooking time will vary, depending on the size and age of the carrots. Add more water if necessary. Drain, reserving liquid.

In a pan, warm the oil over low heat and blend in the flour. Stir continually. Measure the liquid in which the carrots were cooking. Add enough warm water to measure two cups; slowly add liquid to the flour and continue to stir for five minutes. Add ham, carrots, salt, and pepper. Simmer a few minutes and serve hot.

SERVES 4.

Ejotes con Mantequilla

Green Beans with Butter

2 pounds green
beans · 1 cup
water · 1 teaspoon
salt · 1/2 cup
butter · 2 sprigs
parsley, chopped ·
1/4 teaspoon
nutmeg ·
1 teaspoon lemon
juice ·
1/2 teaspoon salt ·
1/4 teaspoon
pepper ·

Wash beans; remove ends and strings if necessary. Snap in two, or if the beans are small, leave them whole. Cover and boil rapidly in one cup of salted water for 20 minutes or until the beans are tender.

Add butter, parsley, nutmeg, lemon juice, salt, and pepper. When the butter has melted, place the beans on a platter and serve hot.

SERVES 8.

For those of us living north of the border, salads are an essential part of the main meal, but this is not true in Mexico. Salads are served in restaurants catering to the American tourists, or in Mexican homes to American visitors, or at special occasions on fiesta days.

Salads are not really necessary to the meal, for the Mexican cook garnishes her plates with olives, chiles, radishes, onions, lettuce, and avocados.

As various fruits are in abundance in Mexico, the natives prefer to eat raw fruit, like papayas, bananas, mangoes, or tuna, which has nothing to do with fish, but is the fruit of the prickly pear cactus. The inevitable portable stand piled high with fresh fruits for sale appears on the various street corners in towns all over Mexico.

Ensalada de Camarones

Shrimp Salad

3 cups canned or cooked shrimp (refer to page 126 for cooking shrimp) · 2 tablespoons vinegar · 2 tablespoons olive oil · 1/4 cup mayonnaise, commercial or homemade · 1/2 teaspoon salt · 1/4 teaspoon pepper · lettuce · 12 radishes, cut like roses for a garnish ·

If shrimps are canned and small, leave them whole. If large, cut them up. Mix with vinegar, oil, mayonnaise, salt, and pepper. Serve in individual salad bowls with lettuce, and garnish with radish roses.

To make radish roses, cut off a little of the top and bottom of the radish. Cut sections of the radish from the tip toward the stem end. Loosen in order that the sections stand out like petals. Refrigerate in ice water until petals curl.

SERVES 6.

Ensalada de Frijol

Bean Salad (pictured on cover)

3 cups cooked
kidney beans ·
1/2 cup chopped
sweet pickle ·
5 hard boiled eggs,
chopped · 3/4 cup
celery, diced ·
1 cup mayonnaise,
commercial or
homemade ·

Drain beans. Add pickle, eggs, and celery. Toss together, lightly. Add mayonnaise and blend. Chill thoroughly. Serve on shredded lettuce.

SERVES 6.

Guacamole

Avocado Salad

A favorite once served in the court of Montezuma, this salad's history goes back long before the coming of the Spaniards to Mexico.

4 ripe avocados ·
1 teaspoon lemon
juice · 1 garlic
clove, chopped
finely · 1/2 large
onion, chopped ·
1/2 cup tomatoes,
peeled and
chopped ·
2 teaspoons canned
jalapeño chiles,
chopped ·
2 teaspoons
parsley, chopped ·

Peel avocados; cut in half to remove seed, and slice in small pieces. Mash the lemon juice with avocados, either with a fork or in the blender. Blend the other ingredients with the avocados. Serve over fresh lettuce leaves.

SERVES 4.

Ensalada de Noche Buena

Christmas Eve Salad

This is a fiesta or special occasion treat. After Christmas Eve Mass or at midnight, a supper is served which traditionally includes this salad.

8 small cooked beets, or a 16 ounce can whole or sliced beets · 4 oranges, peeled · 4 red apples, cored but unpeeled · 4 bananas, peeled · 1 fresh pineapple, peeled and cored, or 1 can (1 pound 14 ounce) pineapple chunks · 3 limes, peeled · 1 cup mayonnaise · 1/4 cup sugar · 1 head lettuce · seeds of 2 pomegranates, or 4 tablespoons cranberries from a can of whole cranberries · 1 cup peanuts, chopped ·

Slice beets, oranges, apples, bananas, pineapple, and limes. Shred the lettuce and put it in the bottom of a large salad bowl. Mix the fruit with the mayonnaise and sugar and arrange over the lettuce.

Garnish the top of the salad with the pomegranate seeds (or cranberries) and the chopped peanuts.

SERVES 8.

Ensalada de Coliflor

Cauliflower Salad

1 small head
cauliflower ·
1 teaspoon salt ·
1 cup water ·
2 tablespoons olive
oil · 1 cup orange
juice ·
2 hard-boiled eggs,
chopped in small
pieces · 1 jalapeño
chile, chopped ·
1 teaspoon ground
mustard ·
1/2 teaspoon leaf
oregano ·
1 teaspoon salt ·
1/2 teaspoon
pepper ·

Separate cauliflower into flowerets and wash thoroughly. Boil rapidly in salted water for 10 minutes. Drain and cool. Place in a salad bowl.

Mix together the oil, vinegar, orange juice, eggs, jalapeño, ground mustard, oregano, salt, and pepper. For best results, put this mixture in a quart jar and shake vigorously. Cover the cauliflower with this sauce and serve.

SERVES 4–5.

Ensalada de Corazones de Alcachofas

Artichoke Hearts Salad

1 pound artichoke
hearts, frozen or
canned ·
4 tablespoons olive
oil · 2 tablespoons
vinegar ·
1 teaspoon ground
mustard ·
1 teaspoon salt ·
1/2 teaspoon
pepper · 4 ounce
can whole
mushrooms ·

Prepare frozen artichoke hearts according to the instructions on the package. Drain and cool. Cut in small pieces; place in a salad bowl. In a jar, shake together the olive oil, vinegar, dry mustard, salt, and pepper.

Cover the artichoke hearts with the dressing and garnish with mushrooms.

SERVES 4–5.

Ensalada de Nueces

Walnut Salad

1 cup walnuts, shelled and chopped · 1/2 cup vinegar · 1 teaspoon salt · 2 stalks celery, chopped · 1 cup canned asparagus tips, drained · 1/2 cup mayonnaise ·

Marinate the walnuts in vinegar and salt for 30 or 40 minutes.

Mix the celery, asparagus, and walnuts with the mayonnaise and serve.

SERVES 3–4.

Ensalada de Hortalizas

Vegetable Salad

3 large potatoes, peeled · 1 teaspoon salt · 1 cup asparagus tips, canned or frozen, chopped · 6 artichoke hearts, canned or frozen, chopped · 4 ounce can mushrooms, sliced · 2 stalks celery, chopped · 1 teaspoon salt · 1/2 teaspoon pepper · 1 cup mayonnaise ·

Cook the potatoes, in enough salted water to cover, for about 20 minutes, until they are tender but not mushy. Drain, cool, and slice in small pieces. Add asparagus and artichoke hearts, drained of any liquid if you are using the canned, to the potatoes, and put in a salad bowl.

Mix in mushrooms, celery, salt, pepper, and mayonnaise. Refrigerate for an hour before serving.

SERVES 6.

los postres y los dulces

14

desserts and sweets

Desserts and sweets were not enjoyed in the court of Montezuma, nor were they known to any of the natives in this hemisphere before the arrival of the Spanish. Sweets were not native to the Spanish either; rather, their introduction into the cuisine was the result of the Moorish domination of Spain, which lasted nearly a thousand years. When the Spanish arrived in Mexico, they brought with them sugar, flour, and spices unknown in the new world.

The Spanish nuns must be given the credit for introducing sweets in Mexico. They specialized, and still do today, in preparing desserts and fancy candies either for gifts or to be sold at fiestas and religious functions.

Although one may be offered a type of candy dessert after the multicourse meal in the early afternoon, confections are more apt to be a "snack" in the late afternoon or early evening.

Polvorones

Mexican Tea Cakes (pictured on cover)

1 cup butter ·
1/2 cup confectioners sugar · 2-1/4 cups sifted flour ·
1/4 teaspoon salt ·
1 teaspoon vanilla ·
confections sugar for rolling ·

Cream butter; add sugar, flour, salt, and vanilla, making a stiff dough. Make into a ball and chill in the refrigerator for several hours. Roll, between hands, into small balls—one inch in diameter.

Bake on a buttered cookie sheet in a 400° oven from 14 to 17 minutes. Remove from oven and immediately roll in confectioners sugar. Cool on wire rack. When cool roll in sugar again.

MAKES ABOUT 5 DOZEN COOKIES.

Arroz con Leche a la Criolla

Creole-Style Rice Pudding

1/2 cup long grain rice · 1 cup water · 2 cups milk · 1/2 teaspoon cinnamon · 1 lemon rind, grated · 1/2 cup granulated sugar · brown sugar · 1 ounce rum ·

Boil the rice in a saucepan in water for five minutes. Drain.

In an ovenproof baking dish, mix together the rice, milk, cinnamon, and lemon rind. Bake in a 425° oven for 10 minutes; then mix in the granulated sugar and bake 10 minutes more.

Remove the dish from the oven and sprinkle with brown sugar. Refrigerate to serve cool. Just before serving, pour rum over rice and light with a match.

SERVES 4.

Arroz con Leche

Rice Pudding

1/2 cup long grain rice · 1 cup water · 1 inch stick cinnamon · 4 cups milk · 1-1/4 cups granulated sugar · 2 egg yolks, lightly beaten · 1/3 cup seedless raisins · 1 teaspoon powdered cinnamon ·

Soak the rice in enough hot water to cover for 15 minutes. Drain and wash well in cold water. Cook in one cup of water with the cinnamon stick until the water is absorbed. Add milk and sugar and cook over low heat for 30 minutes. Remove from the heat. Stir in egg yolks and raisins. Cook over low heat, stirring often, for five more minutes or until the mixture attains a custard-like consistency. Sprinkle with the powdered cinnamon and serve cool.

SERVES 6.

Manjar Blanco

Blancmange

4 tablespoons cornstarch, or 6 tablespoons flour · 1/2 cup granulated sugar · 1 inch stick cinnamon · 1 lemon rind, grated · 1/4 teaspoon salt · 3 cups milk · 1 cup almonds, blanched and finely chopped · 1 teaspoon vanilla ·

Put cornstarch (or substitute flour), sugar, cinnamon, lemon rind, and salt in the top of a double boiler. Slowly stir in milk. Cook over boiling water, stirring constantly, until the mixture is thick and smooth—about five minutes. Cover and cook 15 minutes longer, stirring often. Remove cinnamon stick.

Add vanilla and almonds; pour into molds and refrigerate. Unmold or serve in the molds with your favorite ice cream sauce or fresh fruits.

SERVES 6.

Huevecitos de Faltriquera

Little Eggs in a Pocket

2 cups sugar · 1 cup water · 10 egg yolks, well-beaten · ground cinnamon ·

Stir the sugar and water together until the sugar is dissolved. Bring to a boil. Cover and cook for three minutes. Uncover and cook without stirring another 15 minutes. Be careful not to burn the mixture. Cool.

Add the sugar slowly to the egg yolks, beating continually. When well mixed, bring to a boil over a low fire, constantly stirring until the mixture begins to separate from the bottom of the pan. Cool.

Moisten your hands in cold water and roll the mixture into oval balls the size of small eggs. Roll each one in cinnamon. Serve at once or refrigerate.

SERVES 6–8.

Budín de Elote

Corn Pudding

1 cup fresh corn cut from cob (about 3 ears) · 3 eggs, separated · 1/2 cup (4 ounces) butter (room temperature) · 1/4 cup sugar · 1 cup milk · 1 teaspoon salt · 3 teaspoons bread crumbs · 1/2 cup heavy cream, whipped ·

Blend the corn, egg yolks, and butter in a blender. Mix in by hand the sugar, milk, and salt. Beat egg whites to a peak. Fold the egg whites into the mixture. Pour into a greased one-quart baking dish. Top with bread crumbs.

Bake in a moderate 375° oven for 30 minutes, or until the mixture is dry when a toothpick is inserted in the middle. Serve hot, topped with whipped cream.

SERVES 4.

Quesadillas de Leche de Baja California

Milk Cheesecake from Baja California

3 cups milk · 1 cup light cream · 1 inch cinnamon stick · 2 cups brown sugar · 1/2 cup vanilla wafers, crumbled ·

Cook the milk, cream, cinnamon, and brown sugar over medium heat, stirring continually until thick, to the point where a bit of the mixture forms a little ball when put in cold water. Take from the heat and beat until the mixture forms a paste. Top with the vanilla wafer crumbs. Refrigerate until thoroughly cold for an hour or two before serving.

SERVES 6.

Galletita de Mantequillas

Butter Cookies

1 cup flour ·
1/2 cup sugar ·
4 tablespoons
butter, room
temperature ·
1 teaspoon baking
powder · 1/4 cup
milk · 1 egg,
beaten ·

Combine flour, sugar, butter, baking powder, milk, and egg; mix well. Roll out the dough with a rolling pin until it is about 1/4 inch thick. Cut out the cookies with cookie cutter. Place on a greased cookie sheet, and bake in a 350° oven until lightly browned, about 8 to 10 minutes.

MAKES 2 DOZEN COOKIES.

Mantecadas de Astorga

Astorga Cupcakes

2 cups cake flour,
sifted · 3 teaspoons
baking powder ·
1/2 teaspoon salt ·
1/2 teaspoon
ground cinnamon ·
1/2 cup (4 ounces)
butter · 1-1/4 cups
granulated sugar ·
2/3 cup milk ·
1 teaspoon vanilla ·
4 egg whites ·

Add baking powder, salt, and cinnamon to the sifted flour.

Cream butter; add sugar gradually, continually beating until light and fluffy. Add a little of the flour mixture; then a little milk, Stir after each addition to blend, but do not beat. Add vanilla.

Beat egg whites stiff and fold into batter. Fill greased cupcake pans two-thirds full and bake in a 375° oven 20 to 25 minutes. When cool, serve plain or frost with white frosting.

MAKES ABOUT 2 DOZEN CUPCAKES.

Panetela Campechana

Campeche Sponge Cake

**3/4 cup cake flour, sifted twice ·
5 eggs, separated ·
1/8 teaspoon salt ·
1/2 teaspoon baking powder ·
1 cup sugar ·
1 lemon rind, grated ·
3 tablespoons water · powdered sugar · ground cinnamon · whipped cream (optional) ·**

Sift flour twice and measure.

Beat egg whites to a peak. Add salt and baking powder, and gradually beat in half of the sugar a little at a time.

Beat egg yolks until thick; add remaining sugar, lemon rind, and water; continue to beat until the mixture is thick. Fold in the beaten egg whites and the flour.

Pour into an ungreased 9-inch tube pan and bake at 325° for one hour. Remove from oven and invert the pan. Let the cake stand inverted until cool.

Remove from pan and sprinkle with powdered sugar and cinnamon. May be served topped with whipped cream.

MAKES ONE 9 INCH CAKE.

Compota de Manzanas

Apple Compote

**1 cup sugar · 1 cup water ·
1 tablespoon lemon juice · rind of 1 orange, grated ·
2 pounds apples ·**

In a saucepan, combine sugar, water, lemon juice, and orange rind. Stir over low heat until the sugar dissolves; then bring to a boil for five minutes.

Peel and core apples; cut in quarters. Poach the apples, a few at a time, in the sugar syrup until soft. Place apples in fruit jars; pour remaining syrup over apples and refrigerate before serving.

SERVES 6.

Tortilla Soufflé

Omelet Soufflé

1/3 cup flour ·
1/2 cup granulated
sugar ·
1/4 teaspoon salt ·
1 cup milk · 4 eggs,
separated ·
1/4 teaspoon cream
of tartar ·
1 teaspoon
vanilla ·

In a saucepan, combine flour, sugar and salt. Gradually add milk. Cook over low heat until mixture is thick, stirring continually.

Beat egg yolks until thick. Fold the yolks into the milk mixture and cool.

Beat egg whites until foamy; add cream of tartar; continue to beat until stiff but not dry. Add vanilla and fold egg white mixture into egg yolk mixture.

Pour into an ungreased 1-1/2 quart casserole dish. Bake at 425° about 25 minutes until well browned. Serve hot from the dish in which it was baked.

SERVES 6.

Cajeta

Little Box (Sauce)

1 cup granulated
sugar · 4 cups cold
milk · 1/8 teaspoon
baking soda ·

Cook the sugar over very low heat until almost brown; do not allow it to turn into caramel or burn. Add the milk and baking soda, stirring continually. Bring to a boil and continue to stir until the mixture thickens. Can be kept in glass jars at room temperature for a week, or will keep indefinitely if refrigerated.

Cajeta is somewhat like a butterscotch sauce. In Mexico, it is served on crackers, but you might try some on the ice cream recipes that follow.

MAKES 4 CUPS.

Empanaditas con Almendras

Almond Turnovers

2 cups flour, sifted ·
2 teaspoons baking
powder ·
1 teaspoon salt ·
1/2 cup
all-vegetable
shortening ·
1/2 cup cold water ·
1/2 cup almonds,
blanched and
chopped · 1/2 cup
sugar · 1 teaspoon
ground cinnamon ·
1 egg white ·
1/4 teaspoon
almond extract ·
1/4 cup vegetable
oil ·

Sift flour, baking powder, and salt together. Cut in the shortening with two knives until the mixture resembles coarse crumbs. Add very cold water, one tablespoon at a time, mixing until flour is moistened. Shape into a ball. Roll to about 1/8 inch thickness on lightly floured surface. Cut with a glass or cookie cutter into 2-1/2 inch circles.

Mix together almonds, sugar, and cinnamon. Beat egg white with almond extract until frothy. Stir in the almond and sugar mixture. Place one teaspoon filling on half of each circle. Wet edges to seal. Fry in hot oil, turning once. Drain on paper towels and serve hot.

SERVES 6.

Dulce de Melocotón

Peach Candy

2 cups peaches,
peeled and sliced ·
4 cups granulated
sugar · 1 cup
water · 1/4 cup
coconut, grated ·

Simmer the peaches in a pan over low heat, being careful not to burn them. Add sugar, water, and coconut; simmer until the peaches acquire a jelly-like consistency and the syrup thickens. Pour into a greased pan and chill before serving. Will keep indefinitely in the refrigerator.

MAKES 12–15 SERVINGS.

Dulce de Pasta de Almendras

Almond Candy

1 cup almonds, blanched and slivered · 1 egg white, stiffly beaten · 1/2 cup powdered sugar · 1/4 teaspoon vanilla ·

Mix the almonds with the egg white, sugar, and vanilla. Roll between hands into small balls about one inch in diameter. Place in a buttered baking dish, and bake at 350° for five minutes.

MAKES 8 SERVINGS.

Cocada

Coconut Candy

1 cup granulated sugar · 1/2 cup water · 1/2 cup milk · 4-ounce can coconut, shredded · 4 egg yolks, beaten · 1 inch stick cinnamon ·

Boil sugar in water and milk mixture for 10 minutes. The mixture should be a syrupy consistency. Add coconut and continue to boil slowly for another 15 minutes, but stirring frequently. Cool a little. Then add egg yolks and cinnamon. Bring to a boil and stir continually for 30 minutes. Pour in a buttered baking dish and bake at 325° for 20 minutes. The mixture should be lightly brown. Refrigerate before serving.

SERVES 6.

Ice Cream

Most Mexican cookbooks do not include ice cream recipes, for they contain ingredients not readily available in Mexico. In addition, Mexicans are not big eaters of homemade ice cream, for although the cook will certainly have a blender in her kitchen, she probably does not have an electric ice cream freezer, or a deep-freeze, and the freezer in her refrigerator will be small.

The following ice cream recipes may be frozen, using an electric or hand freezer with ice and ice cream salt, or they may be fast frozen in ice trays in the freezer.

Helado de Bocado

Ice Cream Morsel

8 cups milk · 2 teaspoons vanilla · 1 cup granulated sugar · 10 egg yolks · 4 egg whites, well beaten ·

Bring the milk and vanilla to a boil; add the sugar and let the mixture boil for a few minutes more. Beat the egg yolks in a cup and drop them on top of the hot milk, stirring continually. Simmer until the mixture thickens; remove from the fire and continue beating until it cools. Add the beaten egg whites and freeze.

MAKES 3 QUARTS.

Helado de Café

Coffee Ice Cream

1-1/2 cups granulated sugar · 3 cups light cream · 2 eggs, beaten · 3 tablespoons instant coffee · 1/8 cup hot water ·

Scald the sugar and cream over low heat, but do not boil. Add the beaten eggs, and the instant coffee which has been dissolved in hot water. When the mixture is smooth, remove from the heat and freeze.

MAKES 9 SERVINGS.

Helado de Chocolate

Chocolate Ice Cream

2 cups milk · 2 cups light cream · 4 ounces semi-sweet chocolate · 3/4 cup granulated sugar · 1/4 teaspoon salt ·

Dissolve the chocolate in the milk. Add the cream, sugar, and salt. Boil until the sugar has dissolved and the milk and cream are scalded. Allow to cool before freezing.

MAKES 1-1/2 QUARTS.

Helado de Plátano

Banana Ice Cream

6 ripe bananas · 1 cup granulated sugar · 1 cup water ·

Mash the well-ripened bananas with a spoon.

Boil the sugar and water together until it reaches a thread stage (86°). Allow to cool.

Mix the bananas with the sugar syrup and freeze.

MAKES 6 SERVINGS.

hints to the cook

For the grains of rice to stay white and separated, add a few drops of lemon juice or vinegar to the water.

To revive fresh vegetables, put them, for at least an hour, in ice water to which a few drops of lemon juice or vinegar have been added.

To peel tomatoes easily, drop them in boiling water for two minutes.

To cut onions without crying, keep them submerged in a pan of water while cutting.

To eliminate some of the unpleasant odor from cabbage and cauliflower, add a slice of bread to the water as they are cooking.

Fried potatoes retain a better color if they are sprinkled with flour before frying.

Meringues are better if the egg whites are beaten in brass containers.

Bananas should never be stored in the refrigerator. The cold makes them lose their flavor, and they will spoil easily.

To remove excess salt from anything you have cooked, add a lump of sugar for a few minutes and wait until the sugar begins to dissolve. Remove the lump of sugar and the dish will be perfectly seasoned, as the salt "goes" to the sugar.

Baste your roast in oil before cooking to conserve both the flavor and the juice.

To hard-boil eggs, place eggs in cold water to cover. Bring the water to a boil, remove from the heat, and leave the eggs in the hot water for 30 minutes before removing shells.

It is easier to beat egg whites to the point of snow if a few drops of lemon juice and a pinch of salt or sugar are added to them.

Leftover oil that has been used for frying fish can be kept for seasoning if a few drops of lemon juice are added to it. This removes the fishy taste.

Mayonnaise can be revived by adding a little boiled vinegar to it and beating it vigorously.

Water will not boil over a pan if the top two or three inches of the pan are rubbed with butter.

Egg yolks may be kept more readily if they are placed in a cup (being careful not to break them) with a little cold water. Cover and place in the refrigerator.

Lima beans and peas should not be shelled until you are ready to cook them.

Scales can be removed from fish more easily if the fish are submerged in hot water first.

You can extract twice as much juice from a hot lemon than from one which is cold.

Add a little bicarbonate of soda to preserves made from citrus fruits such as oranges. They will not be as acid or as sugary.

Save the water in which vegetables are cooked to put into soups and sauces. It is very nourishing.

useful information

Almuerzo—means lunch, but usually refers to a mid-morning meal, for the main meal in the middle of the day is the "comida."

Antojitos—a term used exclusively in Mexico referring to little snacks, like tacos, chalupas, and tamales. Usually served in the late afternoon.

Atole—a gruel-like drink with a corn base made with water, masa, sugar, and milk. May be flavored with fruit or chocolate.

Beans—(called "frijoles" in Spanish) dried pinto, red, or kidney beans found in this country as well as in Mexico. Dried black beans and chickpeas are used extensively in Mexican cooking but are difficult to find north of the border.

Blanching—pouring boiling water over food to remove outer covering. Used especially for slipping the skins of nuts like almonds, or for the easy removal of tomato skins.

Blender—a necessary piece of equipment for the Mexican kitchen. The Mexican cook will purée or blend nearly anything from sauces to vegetables.

Cazuela—an earthenware casserole.

Cena—the evening meal, served at 9:00 or 10:00 at night. This is usually a light supper consisting of various types of antojitos.

Cheese—to substitute for Mexican cheese, which is rarely available in this country, use any type of Cheddar. Other good substitutes are Romano, Parmesan, and Monterey Jack cheese.

Chiles—an Indian word which the Spaniards applied to any type of pepper. In Mexico they are called by many names and are a variety of shapes.

To substitute for Mexican peppers or chiles:

ancho chile—resembles bell peppers but usually more peppery; use bell peppers.

poblano chile—green ancho chile; use California chiles if available; if not, substitute bell peppers.

serrano chile—small green pepper that is extremely hot; use any variety of small or red or green hot peppers.

jalapeño chile—the most readily available species of Mexican pepper in this country. Canned or pickled jalapeños may be purchased in your supermarket. If you do have to substitute, use any variety of small red or green pepper.

Chile verde—means "green chili." The sauce as canned commercially in the United States is made from green chile peppers.

Chorizo—hot Mexican sausage.

Cinnamon—Mexican cooks generally use the stick cinnamon variety rather than powdered, and the stick cinnamon sold in that country has a little different flavor than that available in the United States. To substitute in any of the recipes calling for stick cinnamon, approximately one inch stick of cinnamon equals one tablespoon powdered cinnamon.

Comida—the multicourse meal generally served between 2:00 and 2:30 in the afternoon.

Desayuno—means breakfast but usually consists of a continental type of breakfast of tortillas, rolls, and a beverage.

Diced—to cut into small cubes.

Epazote—use dried parsley as a substitute for epazote.

Flores de Calabaza—squash blossoms cooked as a vegetable, and often used as a garnish.

Fricassee—a dish made of chicken, veal, or other meat cut into pieces and stewed in a gravy.

Masa—corn kernels soaked in lime water; then ground as fine as possible. Masa dough is used for making corn tortillas.

Mince—to cut or chop in very small pieces.

Mole—a sauce used with meat and fowl, which is made with chiles and various spices, and which often includes Mexican chocolate.

Nopal—the leaf of prickly pear cactus, with a taste and texture something like green beans.

Peppercorns—the dried berries of the pepper vine.

Poached—a moist heat or steam cooking process. The water should remain just below the boiling point.

Pulque—a drink made from the fermented juice of the century plant. Legend tells us that this drink caused the extermination of the Tolteca nation.

Quesadillas—turnovers made by stuffing unbaked tortillas together with a variety of fillings, pinching the edges together, and frying them golden brown. May be served as antojitos, or with a sweet filling for dessert.

Roux—although not necessarily called by that name, many recipes require a roux. To prepare a roux: melt 2 tablespoons butter in a pan. Blend in 2 tablespoons flour over low heat, stirring for 3 minutes. Slowly stir in 1 cup of milk, which can be scalded previously or used just as it comes from the container. Stir with a wooden spoon continually until mixture thickens and is smooth.

Shallot—a bulbous perennial herb from the onion family, which resembles garlic in flavor. Garlic may be substituted for recipes calling for shallots, or 3–4 shallots equals one medium-sized onion.

Tacos—small tortillas fried to form a semi-circle and stuffed with various mixtures.

Tortillas—thin, round, flat cakes made from corn or wheat flour. Tortillas, served plain, are the bread of Mexico. They are a necessary ingredient for making all types of enchiladas, chalupas, burritos, tacos, and tostados.

Tuna—has nothing to do with the fish family. The fruit of the prickly pear cactus. May be candied, eaten raw with a lemon and sugar, or served for dessert.

conversion table—metric system

All equivalents are approximate.

Mass Weight

SYMBOL	WHEN YOU KNOW	MULTIPLY BY	TO FIND	SYMBOL
oz	ounces	28	grams	g
lb	pounds	0.45	kilograms	kg

EXAMPLES:

1/2 ounce	=	15 grams
1 ounce	=	30 grams
1-3/4 ounces	=	50 grams
2-1/2 ounces	=	75 grams
3-1/2 ounces	=	100 grams

17 ounces (1 pound, 1 ounce) = 500 grams
35 ounces (2 pounds, 3 ounces) = 1 kilogram

3 pounds = 1.3 kilograms
4 pounds = 1.8 kilograms
5 pounds = 2.2 kilograms
6 pounds = 2.7 kilograms
7 pounds = 3.1 kilograms
8 pounds = 3.6 kilograms
9 pounds = 4.0 kilograms
10 pounds = 4.5 kilograms

Volume

SYMBOL WHEN YOU KNOW MULTIPLY BY TO FIND SYMBOL

SYMBOL	WHEN YOU KNOW	MULTIPLY BY	TO FIND	SYMBOL
tsp.	teaspoon	5	milliliters	ml
tbsp.	tablespoon	15	milliliters	ml.
fl oz.	fluid ounce	30	milliliters	ml.
c.	cups	0.24	liters	l.
pt.	pints	0.47	liters	l.
qt.	quarts	0.95	liters	l.
gal.	gallons	3.8	liters	l.

EXAMPLES:

3-1/2 ounces = 1 deciliter
7/8 pint   = 1 demiliter
1-3/4 pints (35 ounces) = 1 liter
1 teaspoon   = 4.9 cubic centimeters
1 tablespoon = 14.8 centimeters
1 cup   = 236.6 cubic centimeters

Temperature (Exact)

SYMBOL	WHEN YOU KNOW	MULTIPLY BY	TO FIND	SYMBOL
F°	Fahrenheit temperature	5/9 (after subtracting 32)	Celsius temperature	C°

EXAMPLES:

Fahrenheit to Centigrade:

85° - 29.4	250° - 121.1
86° - 29.9	300° - 148.8
100° - 37.6	350° - 176.6
150° - 65.5	400° - 204.6
200° - 93.3	450° - 232.2

English Index

A

Almond
  candy, 220
  drink, 19
  eggnog, 13
  pulque, 11
  tamales, 90
  turnovers, 219
almuerzo, 226
ancho chile, 227
Anchovies in vinegar sauce, 5
Antojitos, 226
  definition, 74
Appetizers, 2-5
Apple compote, 217
Artichoke hearts salad, 209
Asparagus
  Roman-style, 202
  with mayonnaise, 201
Atole, 226
  definition, 18
Avocado
  salad (guacamole), 207
  soup, 26
Aztec pudding (chicken), 174

B

Bacon, thick, crisp in green sauce, 134
Banana ice cream, 122
Bass
  baked, 114
  in green sauce, 113
Bean(s), 226
  broth, 43

Bean(s) (cont'd.)
  enchiladas, 79
  green, Castillian-style, 200
  green, in sauce, 201
  green, with butter, 204
  lima, Austrian-style, 203
  Mexican-style, 96
  refried, 95, 196
  salad, 207
  soup, 27
  tacos, 102
  tortillas, Veracruz, 96
  with pork, 59
Bechamel-style sauce, 71
Beef
  (calves) liver soup, 33
  filet, Galician-style, 136
  sirloin, regency-style, 136
  tacos, 103
Beefsteaks
  American-style, 135
  Russian, 134
  with anchovies, 135
Beverages, 10-23
blanching, 226
Black bean soup, 28
Blancmange, 214
blender, 226
Broth
  bean, 43
  "fast made," 44
  Long Alvaradeñor, 42
  without fat, 42
Burritos
  with beans, cheese, and chili filling, 78
  with hamburger, 77
  with sausage and beans, 78

Spanish Index

A

Adobo, 146
Aguacate, sopa de, 26
Ajoaceite, 69
Ajo, sopa de, 29
Albondigas, 137
Almejas, sopa de, 39
Almendras, atole de, 19
Anchoas a la vinagreta, 5
Anillo de atún, 121
Arroz
    a la catalana, 61
    a la mejicana, 46
    blanco, 48
    con camerones, 49
    con jaibas, 61
    con leche, 213
    con leche a la criolla, 213
    con ostiones, 47
    con ostiones, sopa de, 34
    con pescado, 48
    con pollo, 162
    en tomatada, 62
    tropical, 62
    verde, 47
    y jitomate, sopa de, 34
Atole, 18, 226

B

Bacalao
    en cebollado, 116
    en salsa roja, 117
Bagre en salsa de jitomate, 115

Bisteques
    a la americana, 135
    con anchoas, 135
    rusos, 134
Blanco, atole, 20
Budín
    azteca (pollo), 174
    de elote, 215
Burritos
    con chorizo y frijoles, 78
    con frijoles, queso y chiles, 78
    con hamburguesa, 77

C

Cabrito en salsa marinera, 157
Café
    con leche, 23
    licor de, 15
Cajeta, 218
Calabacitas, budín de, 60
Calabaza, sopa de, 30
Caldo
    de frijoles, 43
    de pollo, 43
    largo alvaradeño, 42
    "pronto hecho," 44
    sin grasas, 42
Camarón, canapé de, 8
Camarones
    arroz con, 49
    coctel de, 3
    en frío, 126
    fritos, 127
    sopa de, 39